PRAISE FOR *THE COMPASSION ADVANTAGE*

"Birch's fresh perspective on leadership sheds light on the greater, broader, and more impactful questions leaders need to ask—not just of their teams, but of themselves. With so many points of view being shared today, Birch offers fresh insights that strike the balance between critical thought and practicality. She shares stories, concepts, and practical strategies that lead to stronger, healthier, and more successful teams."

—Carlo Sicoli, director of business development and partnerships, York University's Schulich School of Business

"*The Compassion Advantage* is a captivating read filled with illuminating stories and practical advice about the pursuit of authentic and compassionate leadership. Birch's book delivers deep insight into compassion and selflessness—the way she frames these as learnable, mission-critical competencies and not just desirable personality traits really hit home for me. Birch makes the case for the importance of relational leadership and provides guidance to 'enlightened' leadership practitioners."

—Paul Heinrich, president and CEO, North Bay Regional Health Centre

"An instructive illustration of how to amplify our stories while leading culture with compassion. Birch provides many considered resources, reflections, and methods of implementation. A must-read for leaders of all levels."

—Kurby Court, president and CEO, Calgary TELUS Convention Centre

"Over the past five years, we have learned more about the importance of compassion, empathy, and adapting to live amidst uncertainty. One might argue that these core values have always been important in our personal lives, but often valued less (or even seen as weaknesses) when it comes to the world of leadership. In her book, Birch makes a crystal-clear case as to why now, more than ever, we need to rethink and re-assess our approach to leadership in a postpandemic, economically turbulent age. Her book offers an engaging and entertaining perspective that will help the leaders of today be well prepared to be the leaders of tomorrow. Bringing together core pillars of behaviour, such as leadership, compassion, humility, innovation, and agility—along with actionable insights and real-world examples—Birch charts a clear path to create a more human approach to leadership that nurtures individuals and teams and sets them up for success in an uncertain world that is changing rapidly. This book stands as a crucial guide for leaders transitioning from a prepandemic, twentieth-century mindset to a forward-thinking, twenty-first-century leadership style—essential for mastering the new world of work."

—Dave Coplin, CEO and founder, The Envisioners

"From the opening sentence, I couldn't put *The Compassion Advantage* down! I felt like Birch wrote an autobiography of my personal and professional life—our stories as veteran female leaders are mirror images. You can't live your life with regrets, but I sure do wish *The Compassion Advantage* was available to me as a young professional—that the window(s) had been opened to me earlier. Now I can start putting into practice the lessons learned and become more self-reflective and relational for the last chapter of my career."

—Johanne Bélanger, FCPA, FCA, ICD.D, CEO, Sodexo Canada

"Whether you are a seasoned leader or just newly into management and striving to grow, this book has plenty to offer. Birch has pulled together experiences and leadership gems from some exceptional sources and infused her own insight to give readers plenty to think on. As a senior leader, I am inspired to reflect on my leadership skills

and how I need to adapt and grow to effectively navigate in an ever-changing world. I will consult this book over and over again!"
—Barbara Bruce, CAE, Hon. MRAIC, executive director,
Alberta Association of Architects

"Birch grabs your full attention with her very first sentence. She rejects traditional leadership approaches focused on 'fixing' the individual. Her compassion for both leaders and the difficult job of leading allows the reader to let their guard down to consider Birch's appeal for a new type of relational leadership. Smart, funny, and human, *The Compassion Advantage* inspires the reader to reevaluate why they became a leader in the first place and to continue their growth."
—Lisa Baiton, president and CEO, Canadian
Association of Petroleum Producers (CAPP)

"The release of *The Compassion Advantage* is impeccably timed for leaders caught in the messy middle of disruption and culture change. A refreshingly practical reboot road map for leaders who strive to do better and be better for their teams, customers, and company."
—Louise Taylor Green, retired CEO and CHRO

"Birch is uniquely suited to address what leaders need now, as a CEO, trainer, leadership coach, consultant, and accomplished academic with a PhD in leadership. Few could fill this need better. In *The Compassion Advantage*, she very clearly articulates seven essential practices with a compelling narrative and attainable actions. Great leaders, adequate leaders, and those soon to be leaders will each benefit in their own way by understanding, developing, or solidifying these seven behavioural practices into personal traits. The beauty of anything truthful is that it brings clarity to more than one thing. Birch's book brings clarity to effective leadership and to workplace mental health, with admirable eloquence. *The Compassion Advantage* is an exceptional work that will surely have a positive impact on those that read it, their teams, and their organizations."
—Paula Allen, SVP, Research and Client Insights, TELUS Health

"To manage today's increasingly complex and volatile environment, teams must work together more effectively than ever. This entertaining guide shows how to embrace relational leadership as a different paradigm and provides a practical road map to get you there. If you want to lead successful teams from a place of truth and compassion, this book is for you."

—Dr. Lynn Mikula, president and CEO,
Peterborough Regional Health Centre

The Compassion Advantage stands out in business books. It offers a fresh lens on leadership, balancing big-picture challenges with practical, implementable strategies. A must-have for leaders looking to make a real difference."

—Dr. Vince Molinaro, founder and CEO, Leadership Contract Inc.

"Birch states it matter-of-factly: the only given in today's warp-speed, tech-enabled, multi-agenda world is one thing—*change*. So, with all this change surrounding and confronting us, why would we not need our leaders and leadership to change as well? Using a meaningful mix of research, leader-led case studies, and personal experiences and observations, Birch has built a compelling case for a new form of leadership, one that can be highly personalized yet equally applied—regardless of your job level or sector. I highly encourage anyone striving to be a more effective leader to read this book."

—David Kincaid, founder and chairman, Level5 Strategy

"Birch has nailed it! This book is a must-read for the aspirational leader—thoroughly engaging, thought-provoking, and life-changing. It draws on stories, anecdotes, interviews with leaders, and Birch's extensive consultancy experience and PhD studies, plus it's full of plenty of hands-on, practical advice and exercises to gain a compassionate advantage. Birch shows how a leader can become an ambassador for positivity in and beyond their organization through the seven key practices of successful, relational team leadership. It is no ordinary perspective on offer: this one is highly original, doable, and sustainable."

—Liz Fulop, BA (Hons), PhD, professor emeritus,
Griffith Business School

"Birch's first-hand account of relational leadership practice, in its demonstration of both humour and humility, shows that through a process of greater self-awareness and critical reflection, the growth of necessary 'cultural' intelligence is enabled. I have no doubt that this text will prove to be a must-have for the myriad managers aspiring to embrace a relational mindset and agile ways of being."

—Dr. Ngaire Bissett, creative leadership collaboration consultant, Central Queensland University

"*The Compassion Advantage* forces you to take an unflinching and, yes, painful look at your leadership style by deconstructing with humility, surgically eliminating all the messy bits, and rebirthing a more intuitive, effective, and humane leader. Do the work! Your team and business will thrive."

—Cristine Martin, CEO, INSPIRE Advertising + Design

THE
COMPASSION
ADVANTAGE

THE
COMPASSION
ADVANTAGE

7
PRACTICES TO LEAD STRONGER,
MORE SUCCESSFUL TEAMS

DR. JILL BIRCH

BirchGrove

Published by BirchGrove, Toronto
www.drjillbirch.com

Edited and designed by Girl Friday Productions
www.girlfridayproductions.com

Cover design: Brad Foltz
Project management: Emilie Sandoz-Voyer
Illustrations: Sam Michaels (pages 1, 9, 24, 55, 74, 94, 120, 144, 168, and 183); Clayton Birch (page 161)

ISBN (hardcover): 978-1-7381029-3-8
ISBN (paperback): 978-1-7381029-4-5
ISBN (ebook): 978-1-7381029-1-4

First edition

For Gordon, my northern man

CONTENTS

What's Your Moment of Truth?

Here's one of mine.

How the hell did I end up on my knees in the president's office?

I was new in the job. This was my first one-on-one meeting with the president of the company. Things seemed to be going well. We'd outlined our high-level goals for the upcoming year. We were about to wrap up, and there was *just one more thing . . .*

He wanted me to review the invite list for an upcoming VIP event to make sure we hadn't left anyone out. Together, we walked over to his desk, where he picked up two hundred neatly stacked business cards. Suddenly, like confetti, they spilled out of his hand and all over the floor. I bent down and rushed to start gathering them up. Instead of helping me, he stood over me and watched me pick up the cards. In what I now see as a remarkable tableau, I found myself at the president's feet.

I could feel him just standing above me, his eyes on the top of my head. Why didn't he get down and help me? He was the one who'd dropped the cards, after all. There were so many cards, their bright logos taunting me as I collected them. The moment seemed to go on forever, and I felt mortified and powerless. I sensed that the president was distancing himself from such a menial task as a way to let me know where I stood in the pecking order. His actions (or lack thereof) left no doubt about who was in charge.

The mental image of being on my knees and handing the cards to the president is forever burned in my mind. It was a *moment of truth.* A moment when I questioned not only his behaviour, but also my own. Why hadn't he just done the human thing and helped? And why had I let him assert that kind of power over me? I left that encounter asking myself, *Does it always have to be this way? And if it doesn't, how can I change things?*

And I realized that I was not alone. Far from it. This scene plays out over and over every day in countless organizations around the world. It may not always look the same. Sometimes, the boss has taken credit for someone else's great idea. Or maybe they've singled someone out in a meeting for asking a question that threatens the balance of power.

What I learned from this encounter is that when you experience a moment of truth, it's vital to deconstruct it and then develop practices to ensure you become a different kind of leader.

• •

The business card story was a moment of truth that made me rethink everything I had learned about leadership. In the old days, I would have let that moment pass. But what I felt that day laid bare the lie I had been telling myself. Up until that moment, my internal story was that I was a hardworking, deferential leader, a chameleon who intuited what an organization—and its CEO—needed and could change my colours to suit the moment. But there was a problem. Over time, this story blocked me from standing up for what *I* believed in.

I was stuck. But I was lucky.

What helped me become "unstuck" was studying leadership as a PhD student in Australia. Once in the program, I began questioning almost everything I'd learned in the previous thirty years. Like many in North America, my schooling had followed the trajectories of both positive and negative leadership stories, from CEOs Tim Cook of Apple to Elizabeth Holmes of Theranos. For too long, stories of heroes and villains, angels and devils have shaped not only how we think about leadership but also how we behave as leaders. Down under, I found myself reading very different leadership books with titles like *Leadership for the Disillusioned* and *The Witch Doctors*, which suggested that contemporary leadership norms and corporate consulting often did more harm than good.

It was eye opening and alarming. I'd been a CEO. And I'd been a consultant. I'd had the good fortune to run multimillion-dollar business units, develop international partnerships, and forge relationships that enabled me to achieve success. As a consultant, I'd facilitated leadership programs, coached executives and teams, developed corporate leadership universities, and designed strategies to help organizations realize their visions. But the PhD shook me to my core. It forced me to face a number of painful moments of truth. As I mulled over mistakes I could have avoided and incidents I could have managed better, I realized I needed a concrete set of practices to guide me.

I clearly remember the day I stumbled upon the term *relational leadership*. I was staying at the home of Ngaire Bissett, my thesis advisor in Australia. It was my first visit of many. We were preparing dinner when she asked me what I wanted to research, and I blurted out, "You know, what I really want to do is hold a mirror up to leadership, to improve how leaders are developed."

She stopped cutting carrots and locked me with her piercing eyes. "Jill," she said, "it's not about holding up a mirror; it's about looking out a window. It's not about the leader; it's about how they relate with others."

My head began to spin. I felt like a five-year-old who'd just been told Santa didn't exist. In North America, the mirror is everything in leadership. Designing leadership interventions is about creating moments of perfection. Individual perfection, that is. Each competency, every psychometric tool, all the "developing your leadership brand" classes share a common theme. They're obsessed with "fixing" the individual leader rather than helping the leader develop healthy relationships.

They are all about breaking down and building up the person staring back at you in the mirror. Yes, there's teamwork in those sessions, but there's not nearly enough of the guiding principles we need today. Suddenly I saw it all so clearly. I knew it was time to smash the mirror and replace it with a window. I needed to help leaders see the bigger picture by looking through the eyes of others. I tossed out everything I thought about leadership and got to work. I had found my North Star.

• •

After five years of researching a PhD in relational leadership, I was ready to share what I'd learned with other leaders. The system I developed not only supported a new model of leadership but was also designed to help organizations drive profitability.

My husband, Gordon, described these years of research as my "Frankenstein Period." While working full-time as a CEO, I "operated on myself," experimenting with dozens of new ways to think about how we lead. I learned that changing how we lead is harder than leading change itself. But I also learned that changing how we lead makes it easier to lead change. Did I go crazy? Yes. Was it worth it? Completely.

• •

Whether you're a seasoned veteran or an aspiring leader, my goal in writing this book is to help you avoid my mistakes. Over the years I'd had a lot of weird things happen to me. My son Clayton calls it the "Jill Factor." Whether it was getting Krazy Glue in my eye before a key meeting in Singapore, having my five-inch heel come off (and get stuck in the grass) as I hosted the mayor at a garden party, or asking a deputy minister if I could hang up her coat only to find out it was a dress (!), shit happened to me.

This was the semifun, lighter side of the Jill Factor, but there was also a darker side. I have been fired, restructured, sacked, or "in transition"—whatever you want to call it—three times in my career. I don't care what any outplacement advisor says—that's a lot of heartache, a lot of soul-searching, and a whole lot of networking. But it taught me the value of never losing sight of those who reached out and never to be surprised by those who didn't.

Throughout all these experiences, I have found that what gets named in our lives becomes our "life." I had assumed this mantle of adversity with gusto and wore the Jill Factor proudly. I was the comeback kid. A single parent for nineteen years, I was the one who would somehow wheedle my way out of tough situations, and I was lucky because I have a great family, friends and colleagues, and a solid track record of achievements. What I was yet to learn was that lying beneath this calm steeliness were untold stories that belied the mask I wore, exposing vulnerabilities that I could confront only now as a PhD student.

To be honest, I hadn't viewed my life as either a well-planned path or a dead end of destruction. Life and work, work and life were just the contents of the blender I lived in, and as an old boss of mine said, "Once in a while, someone presses the *pulse* button to make things more interesting." My business world, my leadership world, and my personal world were that mélange. I saw myself much like one of my favourite cartoon characters, Wile E. Coyote, gingerly leaping from one powder keg to the next, often right before it exploded.

My perspective changed dramatically as a result of two powerful moments of truth.

The first occurred during a Skype meeting with my advisors, when I embarrassingly realized how ignorant I was of leadership theory. Now I know what you are thinking: *Leadership theory? Let me run for the hills!* But let me ask you, How often have you made the same missteps over and over again, like I did? You beat yourself up, wonder why you didn't learn from the mistake, and then, like so many leaders, you get busy. Life moves on. You make the same mistakes again, and the cycle of doubting yourself deepens.

What I learned from this moment was that it was my very lack of knowledge about leadership theory that prevented me from seeing trouble long before it arrived and caused me to botch the execution of strategies and privilege, the vantage point I assumed I had as a senior executive. By applying these new theories, I was able to develop the seven relational practices that will help you in your leadership evolution.

A second moment of truth occurred when my dad made a speech at our wedding. Hank was a man of profound thought who rarely spoke. But that day, as he looked at me, his fifty-five-year-old daughter, now bride (yes, there is hope for everyone), he remarked to the room that there had been a pattern in my life that he'd witnessed. He said that I had used moments of challenging, often gut-wrenching circumstances (my powder kegs) to my advantage—turning them into "stepping stones." I'd never really thought about it like that. But that's what moments of truth do. They help you reconcile the past and recalibrate new behaviours. Hank had opened a *window* for me. That was some wedding gift! I saw how I had been simply *mirroring* the leadership cosmos—in all that this meant—being tough, decisive, charismatic, powerful, successful, in control, someone to be feared. With Dad's two words, "stepping stones," I reevaluated pretty much everything I had held as true.

With time, I was able to hammer my practical experiences into the building blocks of my academic research. It took five years and five residencies in Brisbane to snap the patterns of behaviour I had developed over such a long period and to rethink what leadership was all about. And isn't it interesting that after all that study and research, it was Hank's words that helped me make that last decisive turn? Finally I was able to shift from the metaphor of powder kegs and move toward the stepping stones of this different, new life.

As I was to learn, moments of truth like these profoundly change how you think, how you live, and how you lead.

From where I sit now, I see that it took me too much time to realize I had been "putting on" and "taking off" leadership behaviours much like I would a pair of jeans. If the day called on me to become a charismatic leader, I'd turn on the charm. Innovation required? No problem. I'd stay up all night researching the latest trends to look like I was on top of things the next day. When other days demanded I become exacting, my VPs called me the "purple pen," due to my brutal "tweaking" of documents they'd already worked on for countless hours. On all these occasions I felt I was bringing my best self to work. I was motivating, influencing, and cajoling the team to achieve results, get projects across the finish line, and generally keep the board happy.

Like I'm sure you do, too, as I'd get ready to head into work each day, I'd run through the day's goals, meetings, areas of focus for the team, and decisions needing to be made. When I headed home at night, I'd be frustrated that I hadn't accomplished many of the things I'd set out to do that morning. My brother, Glenn, has a name for this endless noise: he calls it "incoming." It's the zinger email that demands your immediate attention, the boss calling you with a new assignment, or a team member who stops at your door and asks, "Have you got a minute?"

But then it dawned on me. Those day-to-day realities are not wasted distractions; *they are what leadership is all about.* It's not all that often I hear from leaders that there is nothing they love more than a full day of interruptions, juggling priorities, and hairy problems. I remember feeling overwhelmed by the sheer volume of "incoming" combined with politics and power games that had me worn out and worn down. But looking back, I realized my greatest successes rested in forming, cultivating, and sustaining relationships that advanced others' causes and removed everyday roadblocks. I finally got it: *leadership is a way to be and not a thing to do.*

As you read ahead, my goal is that the *window will open.* You'll become more self-aware and compassionate toward others. You'll also be able to read the room faster, rally people around a common cause, and battle those inner voices that may be eating away at your confidence. Your decision-making will improve because it will be fed by the perspectives of those around you. They will trust you more—and you will trust them.

Many leaders I work with confess that they just can't find the time to develop themselves. They tell me they're busy fighting fires and dialing down the drama—which are the two strongest tip-offs that they actually need to develop themselves! Devoting time to enhance your leadership capabilities isn't being selfish. It turns out that by making a date with yourself to explore new ideas, connect with others, and learn more about your industry, you will become a great role model who inspires others to do the same.

To be sure, you've learned a lot over the past few years: navigating the pandemic; forging ahead in equity, diversity, and inclusion; and collaborating with multiple generations. Now is the time to maximize those experiences to move ahead in your career, to demonstrate the behaviour that will distinguish you from others, and to undertake leadership work with a higher standard of care for people in your community and beyond.

Through a combination of extensive research, supporting leaders in my current practice, and conducting interviews with dozens of renowned CEOs and luminaries who have seen it all, I've gained insights that can help you too. By the time you finish reading, you'll be inspired to become more self-reflective and more relational, and you'll have developed a strategy to bulletproof your career. So let's get to it.

CHAPTER 1

How to Be a Relational Leader

A DEFINITION OF *RELATIONAL LEADERSHIP*

When I talk to people about relational leadership, most say, "I'm already a relational leader. I'm much kinder and nicer to people than other leaders I've worked with." While it's great that people are treating each other better than they used to, these endearing qualities have little to do with relational leadership.

So let's begin at the beginning. What is relational leadership? After five years of PhD research and inhaling countless academic articles, the definition of *relational leadership* that I created for myself is as follows: relational leadership is an emergent, cocreated process that gives us the ability to see a situation through another's eyes. This isn't a style or a fad—it's a way of behaving that enables you as a leader to make accelerated and super-informed decisions fed by many perspectives. It creates opportunities for teams to find common ground much faster and act without making so many missteps along the way.

In a nutshell, relational leadership is seeing through the eyes of others to get to the right insight at the right moment to help you make the right decision. As they say in Quebec, it's all about being a master of "*le timing.*" Simple, right? But not so fast. To get to the finish line, leaders need to fuse two core skills. The first skill is innate in every successful leader I've ever worked with. It's the ability to jump into action. What I've observed, however, is that many leaders put too many eggs in the action basket. They're so busy diving from issue to issue, project to project, and fire to fire that they forget to harness the second skill—and that's what gets them into trouble.

Because today's action heroes also need to reflect *while they are in action.* Before a decision or judgment is made, leaders need a practice that will help them crystallize past experiences—of themselves and others. They then need to be like CNN's Wolf Blitzer, commanding their own situation room, where they gather and assess data, process emotion, and parse out events in real time. Lastly, and most vitally, leaders need to frame past and real-time experiences into future stories that have a moral—whether it's the surprise victory, the harebrained scheme that worked, or the one that got away. Leaders who intentionally shape stories empower healthy, thriving cultures.

In our fast-paced world, relational leadership helps us take the pauses needed before we make rash decisions or rush to judgment. If you can fuse action and reflection, you will have created a brand-new superpower for yourself.

What does relational leadership look like in action? Here are a few examples:

I was facilitating a session for a troubled leadership team, and one brave person shared that she was at the end of her rope—with them! Hard as she tried, she couldn't get her colleagues to focus on a problem that had been affecting *all of them* for months. By having the courage to give words to her long-simmering feelings, she changed the team dynamic that day. A couple of her colleagues looked down, embarrassed, as they recognized their contributions to their colleague's misery. They apologized publicly. I was heartened to watch members of the team come together over the lunch break to work out how to fix the problem.

In another session, I was working with a multigenerational board of directors who couldn't see eye to eye. I sensed a common problem that many boards—and organizations—face. The twenty- and thirty-year-olds were rolling their eyes when the fifty- and sixty-year-olds spoke. I could almost hear them thinking, *Here we go again, another lecture on how it was so much better in the old days.* In turn, older board members were dismissive of younger members, convinced they didn't have enough experience to weigh in on complex board matters.

This deteriorating situation had eroded trust and caused paralysis. Coordinating with the board chair and CEO ahead of time, we decided to address the elephant in the room. We started with the facts: we acknowledged the significant age difference in the room. You could feel the tension subside *just by calling it out.* Next, rather than imposing a method to address the chasm, we asked board members what *they* felt would be a good way to help them find common ground. They decided that an "ask me anything" exercise would be a great way to break the ice. Seventy-year-olds asked why the twenty-five-year-olds weren't responding to their preferred way of communicating, which was email. Thirty-year-olds asked fifty-year-olds why they prevented them from leading committee work. Some questions poked fun, some were serious, but you know what, each question opened the door a crack to build understanding and trust. At the cocktail party that night, the generations were more comfortable mixing and mingling, a result of their heartfelt conversations.

What we learn from these situations is that to be a relational leader means you have to be a courageous leader, someone who is able to make the first moves and knows they will be the right moves. That takes guts. Confronting people with their behaviour is risky business. You could end up getting burned. And that's why it's so important to develop a set of practices that will help you take on whatever difficult situation you may find yourself facing.

Like an Olympic athlete, you need to train hard in three skills that are what I've come to call the 3 Ps. The first discipline is to *pause* before you leap headfirst into something; the next is having the patience to *plan* out what needs to be done and in what order, and the third is the rigour to *prepare* for eventualities.

Pausing helps you gain clarity. It gives you the necessary distance to step back and see a challenge for what it is rather than something riddled with assumptions and biases. It's during this phase that you want to arm yourself with the good questions. Planning means working out the concrete steps you need to take to address or resolve a situation.

Preparing helps you identify the most plausible path forward. It's the step that helps you anticipate people's reactions as you begin to course correct. As you go through the seven practices in this book, each one will provide you with a moment to practice these three simple steps—to pause, plan, and prepare.

The glue holding all of this together is the quality of the relationships you form and strengthen every day. Even the best-planned project is going to have its hiccups. And where do those hiccups come from? It's usually not the technology. It's not the expertise of the people around you. If you have problems, it's usually because you haven't invested enough time in getting to know the people around you.

• •

The great German film director Werner Herzog once said, "Asking a deep question is sometimes more important than getting a straight answer."[1] Relational leadership prompts leaders to ask deep questions that start with "how." Most leaders funnel their attention to questions that start with "why," "who," and "what." This is where this new way of leading radically departs from other methods. Asking *how* questions unlocks new ways of seeing, doing, and thinking about things. You'll find that posing questions like "How are you feeling about this project?" or "How can we come at this differently?" or the inevitable "How did it come to this?" will get you to the truth faster.

Relational leading is a changemaker. Because it engages all our senses, it enables us to attack complex problems with greater understanding of and sensitivity to the perspectives of those around us. We are no longer on autopilot, dictating what we think is best. We are

reading the room, listening, observing people's body language and reactions, and incorporating those perceptions into our thinking.

The other huge bonus to becoming more relational as a leader is
that as teams grow stronger, more committed, and innovative, companies thrive. Profits grow. It's been documented that relational leadership produces happier, healthier, and more productive workplaces. A
relational leader makes their organization a better place and sets it up
for a stronger future.

IT STARTS WITH YOU

Early on, when I shared my ideas with Don Tapscott, a renowned leadership expert himself, he threw up his hands, saying, "I won't even pick
up a book with 'leadership' in the title . . ." Don was expressing the
frustration I encountered over and over as I interviewed leaders for
the book: while there has been a lot of stuff written about leadership, it
hasn't evoked the kind of change required to meet the demands of the
twenty-first century.

Don had just written the prescient *Blockchain Revolution*, and
toward the end of that book, he writes that a new way of leading is
required to thrive in the Bitcoin era: "We need a Declaration of
Interdependence"[2] in order to speed up the human transformation
that would be required to keep up with technology and disruption.
He went on to say that leaders need "a strong and steady barreling forward." In short, leaders need to slow down, see the bigger picture, and
be collaborative, but they also need to move fast and maybe break a
thing or two along the way.

It was here I saw my opening.

Exploring how leaders can successfully navigate these two pow-
erfully oppositional forces—facilitating mutual reliance, yet at the
same time going for broke—forms the foundation of this book. In the
twenty-first century, we need to succeed at both.

The fuckups you'll read about at Better.com, Nutrien, and WeWork
demonstrate the downside of *barrelling* as a leadership principle on its
own. It turns out barrelling only gets you so far. Achieving aggressive

results may be the order of the day, but bad leadership has a cost—to the company's bottom line, its reputation, and its employees. That's why it's vital for leaders to develop the capabilities that lift the hearts and minds of people as much as they drive strategy and results. The two are no longer polarizing agents. They are mutualizing forces. The question is, How do we become skilled relational leaders?

UNDERSTANDING THE CHALLENGES

Changing your leadership style can't start until you confront the dragons of your leadership past. This means we must courageously face up to the behaviours that get us into hot water or may have destroyed relationships. We also need to confront the bad influences of other leaders we have worked with in our careers. It's all too easy to start copying those bad behaviours—and before you know it, you've become the bad boss. Failing to acknowledge and address behaviours that are holding you back and not recognizing poor leadership behaviours in others are what prevents many from attaining that next promotion or—worse yet—causes them to be fired.

Don't be the leader that shrugs and tells themselves, "That's just who I am. Can't do much about it." As I was to learn, you can do a lot about it! As you think about your leadership behaviour, check it against the seven deadly derailers that have ended many a promising career.

The first is one that has plagued organizations since the dawn of time: it's the *asshole syndrome*, where really smart people believe that you're the one who is privileged to work with them—not the other way around. They're arrogant, they're terrible listeners, and they use their power to bully people into submission. A term we hear a lot these days is "tone at the top," which refers to leaders who set a bad tone by being completely out of touch with those they work with.

Then there's *superman disorder*. You'll know you have this dreaded affliction when you experience a sense of euphoria, thinking you have "all the answers" and that the path ahead is clear.

There are the *fumblers*, who drop the ball. Leaders who can't execute put their team in horrible predicaments. These leaders impose their will on others, establish tight directives, move up timelines, and set unrealistic goals. To cut corners, they start doing the work themselves (big mistake), pushing others aside. They rely too heavily on their own information sources and experiences, believing them to trump those of others.

Some leaders take great pride in being *multitaskers*. Often the source of mayhem, these leaders have so many balls in the air that it's just a matter of time before one of them drops. There's been a lot written recently about the "busyness badge" and people competing to be busier than everyone else. Ironically, a *Harvard Business Review* study found that the more we multitask, the worse we are at our job.[3] The multitasking leader is distracted, fails to ask the right questions, and misses important details.

Are you a *micromanager*? No one likes to be told how to do their job. When people aren't free to do the jobs they were hired to do, they don't feel trusted—and this negatively impacts decision-making, confidence, and morale. You'll know you're guilty of micromanagement if you hear watercooler talk about there being too much red tape, decision bottlenecks, and infighting where people blame each other. Experts believe one of the main factors of the Great Resignation of 2021 was that people were leaving bosses who were breathing down their necks. One of the toughest things that happens when we earn a promotion is leaving our old job behind. If you were great at sales, for example, and one day find yourself vice president of sales, your natural proclivity is to go to your comfort zone—sales—rather than coaching and mentoring the team.

You'll know the leader who has a bad case of *rearview-mirror-itis* as the one who constantly reminds everyone of the "good old days" and how much better things were when life was simpler, when everyone knew what to do. These are the people who tell you, "Oh, we tried that ten years ago and it didn't work; there's no way it would work now." These are the kind of leaders who wait you out and wear you down.

Then there are the *walking zombies*, who rest on past success, unable to pick up on the signs of the times. Their failure to continually learn and reinvent themselves makes them a real barrier to progress. There's no room for people to stand in place these days; you have to be looking ahead—and getting out ahead—if you're going to stay relevant.

Now that we've identified the derailers, we can begin the work of doing something about them. As you might expect, my seven relational practices are the keys to getting past these obstacles. For starters, reflect on the last few months of work and any roadblocks or hurdles you experienced. Ask yourself whether any of these seven derailers might have prevented you from giving your best. By the end of this book, you'll have the tools to change those.

UNDERSTANDING THE LANDSCAPE

Do you think there's a correlation between a record number of leaders being escorted out the door in 2023 and their lack of knowledge about how leadership is changing? According to the CEO Turnover Report, exits are up 49%, the highest total for a single month on record since the report was begun in 2002.[4] Leadership is evolving, and in order to stay relevant, leaders must understand the seismic shifts happening in the workplace.

SHIFT 1: POST STRONG RESULTS AND SHOW THAT YOU ARE A WORK IN PROGRESS

Organizations everywhere are seeking to professionalize leadership.

It's not good enough anymore for someone to blow through their targets and assume they will get the nod for that next VP role. Selection committees today want to know what you've learned from the mistakes you've made in your career. They want to see what kind of collaborator you are. They want to know whether you've had a coach— and even more importantly, what kind of coach *you* are. They want you to demonstrate that you courageously took on assignments that you might not have had much experience in but that you emerged as a master.

Significantly, they want to see where you have been proactive in developing yourself outside of work. They want to know whether you've travelled the world and what you've learned. They're looking for volunteer experiences in your community and industry association. They want to know which board you chair or sit on. They want to know what conferences you have attended and when the last time was that you participated in a leadership development program. Selection committees are looking for someone who makes the time to grow themselves both inside and outside of work.

Is that you?

SHIFT 2: LEAD THROUGH CHANGE AND SHOW YOU CAN CHANGE

The second shift is that organizations are on the lookout for leaders who are both activists and advocates for change. These days there are as many different kinds of change as there are ways to look at a problem. Many of the leaders I work with tell me they struggle to lead and manage change. The first question I ask is, "What kind of change are you dealing with?" Is it first-order change, where you need to tinker with existing systems? Is it second-order change, where you need to dramatically transform or disrupt an array of products or services?

Think about the different ways you might approach these different kinds of change—you sure wouldn't approach them the same way, would you? But for many leaders, change appears as an amorphous blob; it all looks the same. Don't fall into that trap. Deconstruct the change. Get to know it inside and out.

And just as there are many different kinds of change, there are as many different kinds of problems within that change. Let's look at three of them. Paradoxes are problems where leaders find themselves embroiled in self-contradiction. Think of the paradoxes we experience in technology, where a new system promises to simplify our lives but actually complicates it. Anyone who has installed an enterprise-wide system will know much pain before they realize the gain. Knowing this, how should they move ahead, especially when it comes to keeping the team's spirits up while coaching them along the way?

A dilemma is another kind of problem where there are difficult choices to be made between two or more alternatives—and sometimes, each alternative is equally unpleasant or undesirable. Think about how many leaders have had to make the tough decision between killing a project that is off the rails and investing more into it to see it through. You can't recoup those sunken resources, but what if just a little more effort pays off? These are the kinds of dilemmas that even the most skilled leader agonizes over. Knowing when to walk away is just as important as knowing when to hunker down.

Wicked problems have no clear answers. Companies around the world are working to stave off climate change, create a more just culture, or give back to their communities, but often one solution causes other problems to creep in. The wicked problem is the antagonist of our times. Seeing alternatives and cleverly maneuvering around and through them will be one of the most valuable skills you can develop as you evolve your leadership.

As we saw in my earlier example about the board who was struggling with intergenerational relationships, for the first time ever, organizations have five generations working together under one roof. And that means multiple and differing interpretations of what it means to "lead well" and "work hard." Think of your own workplace and the composition of traditionalists (seventy-six to ninety-nine years old), baby boomers (fifty-seven to seventy-five years old), Generation X (forty-one to fifty-six years old), millennials (twenty-six to forty years old), and Generation Z (twenty-five and younger). Economic pressure has caused many traditionalists and boomers to hold off retirement, while the revolution in the workplace (as a result of the pandemic) has caused many Gen Xers, millennials, and Gen Zers to rethink how they want to work.

According to generational expert Giselle Kovary, different generations have different relationships with authority.[5] A fallout of the intergenerational workplace is that people aren't in step with each other. A relational leader is highly attuned to the needs of each of these generations. They must be equally aware that labelling or pigeonholing generations into stereotypes can backfire. You may think this means understanding the differences between how a forty-year-old and a sixty-five-year-old perceives the workplace, but a *New York Times* article recently cited that thirty-seven-year-olds are now getting the "eye roll" from exasperated twenty-three-year-olds who want to run the office.[6]

Are you the change master your organization needs right now?

SHIFT 3: HARNESS THE POWER OF TECHNOLOGY AND SHOW THE FLEXIBILITY TO LEARN NEW WAYS OF DOING THINGS

When I speak to leaders, I ask them a simple question: "On a scale of 1 to 5, where would you rank your understanding of AI, the metaverse, digital twins, and Bitcoin?" Most give themselves a 2. It's time they learned to become digital leaders.

A McKinsey study recently reported that not enough leaders have engaged deeply with technology, and that without a more sophisticated way to connect the dots within the business, its strategy, and new technologies, executive teams and board members are struggling.[7] And if *they're* struggling, that means we all will. This learning gap leaves leaders and their organizations vulnerable. Leaders need to come clean about where their own gaps lie; they need to quickly embed data analytics experts in their own departments rather than consulting with someone three floors up in IT. Once they get a handle on their *own* tech strengths and weaknesses, they then need to assess and close skill gaps on the team.

Companies are now seeking leaders who have a firm grasp of how to harness technology to drive new revenue, improve business efficiencies, speed time to market, and optimize costs. Getting ourselves ready for this new world means that we all need to become much more tech savvy. Bragging that your five-year-old is in a coding class doesn't count. I'm not saying you have to get a degree in computer science, but keeping up to date is nonnegotiable for those who want to lead today.

How proficient are you when it comes to advances in technology?

SHIFT 4: BECOME A PERFORMER AND SHOW THAT YOU ENJOY IT

Technology and the pandemic brought another change that leaders weren't prepared for: leaders need to become both better performers and better broadcasters. Hybrid work is here to stay. In response to this, leaders need to significantly improve their ability to read the room—or the *Hollywood Squares* tiles on Zoom. Leaders must significantly enhance their skills when it comes to engaging teams virtually and face to face. They need to become mini versions of Anderson

Cooper, looking confidently into their webcam. To do that, they must dive down deep into their tool kit to be able to improvise on the spot, communicate, facilitate, listen, ferret out hunches, and mine the intel of employees working closest to customers. In addition, leaders need to develop greater empathy so that they can be on the lookout for signs of burnout and anxiety.

Are you that leader?

SHIFT 5: REINVENT THE WORKPLACE AND SHOW OPENNESS TO INNOVATION

Another "gift" of the pandemic is the unprecedented change in how people view work. Terms like *mass resignation* and *quiet quitting* only begin to scratch the surface of what leaders are contending with in order to keep their best people and attract talent. This means leaders need to arrive at mutually created responses to how the new world of work will shape work lives. How many times did we see leaders send out edicts for return-to-the-office dates only to get the response from employees, "Ah, I don't think so"?

Understanding others' motivations and needs is essential to creating a happy workplace that hums. We need to put more focus on the concept of *workspaces* (meaning, anywhere) rather than *workplaces*. A Planterra study found that 60% of employees said working from home had improved their health.[8] A whopping 86% of those surveyed said they were satisfied with remote work, with only 20% indicating they wanted to go back to work full-time. Flatter organizations and the democratization of information compel leaders to demonstrate greater compassion and more active listening. Yet these new forms of deep collaboration have left some leaders feeling threatened and on the defensive.

Are you one of them?

Evaluate Your Performance

So, let's end with a practice run on evaluating your performance. In this chapter, we've identified trends and derailers that could have an impact on your career prospects. Let's dive into examining the trends affecting your industry and evaluate derailers that may be setting you back.

Now that you've had time to consider that current state of leadership, take a moment and ask yourself these questions:

- What are the top three trends affecting your sector and how are they impacting your organization?

_____

_____

_____

- Now think about the different kinds of leadership that will be required as a result of these forces. How ready are you to take them on?

_____

_____

_____

- On a scale of 1 to 5 (5 being the highest), how would you rate your tech savvy?

_____

_____

_____

- What do you need to become more tech savvy?

_____

_____

_____

- How are you adapting, and helping others to adapt, to changing ways of working?

_____

_____

_____

- If you saw any of the derailers in your leadership, which ones were they?

_____

_____

_____

- When and why do those behaviours pop up?

_____

_____

_____

- When you think about leaders who are "doing it right" these days, what do you notice about their behaviour?

CHAPTER 2

_____

_____

_____

Practice Becoming More Self-Aware

Whenever I start, I'm always amazed. That wasn't so bad!

—Frank Gehry, architect

Becoming a better leader starts with building greater self-awareness. And greater self-awareness is about owning your leadership experiences—the good, the bad, and the ugly. When I meet leaders who have derailed, are "stuck" or "in denial," it's a clue they haven't really dug down deep to get to the heart of their experience. These leaders are telling themselves a story that is often filled with excuses, finger-pointing, and blame of others. Our experience silently shapes our attitudes, behaviours, and performances every day on the job. Ignore them at your peril: you will never change. It's only when we work with our experiences that we can change the story we tell ourselves—and others. This is where true self-awareness begins. And that self-awareness results in not only greater leadership but a healthier company. Added bonus: studies have revealed a direct correlation between high employee self-awareness and strong financial performance.[9] So there is much to be gained by doing this work.

When I'm in conversations with leaders about their level of self-awareness, I'm often met with a shrug and the comment "You know, I'm always working on myself." But what I *hear* and what I *see* are often at odds with each other. Good intentions don't amount to much. Promises are broken. Words don't match actions. People forget. They get busy. Failure to develop greater self-awareness means nothing will ever change. Not us, not our team, not our organizations.

But there's a problem here. Even with all the coaches and psychometric tests, we don't seem to be making much headway in this area. In a Hay Group research study, a mere 19% of women and 4% of men exhibited self-awareness.[10] A rather shocking statistic that means there's still much work to do. Another study found that teams with a low degree of self-awareness are less than half as effective as teams that are highly self-aware.[11]

There's good reason to awaken our inner selves: people don't leave their organizations; they leave bad bosses—will *you* be that bad boss someday? The more self-aware you are, the more confident and creative you will be. And with this, you're also likely to get more promotions.

Let's be honest: sure, we all have stories where we exhibited strength, but each of us also has stories when things went off the rails. They become our hidden stories. We may feel ashamed, embarrassed, regretful, or filled with remorse. Left to fester, these stories can become toxic because we failed to resolve them or learn from them.

When we don't pay attention to our stories and fail to learn from them, we suffer, and so does everyone around us. Some of us may be given a second chance, others are shown the door. Or you may find yourself paralyzed, going through the motions, acting fulfilled and happy. These are miserable places to be, especially for extended periods of time. This chapter is designed to help you explore your leadership purpose story and then provide you with the tools to turbocharge your self-awareness. These new practices will not only help you *stand out* but also support you to *stand up* for your values as a courageous, humble, and compassionate leader.

‥

First, a note: It may seem contradictory that we're starting with self-awareness and looking inward when relational leadership is all about seeing and inviting in other people's perspectives, but stronger relationships begin with a stronger understanding of self. By knowing your own strengths and weaknesses, you will better be able to engage with others.

There are two ways we want to think about self-awareness. The first is your level of internal self-awareness, where you understand your values, passions and aspirations, and impact on others. Becoming more internally self-aware means getting a better handle on emotions, motivations, desires, and why we react to the world the way we do. The second type, external self-awareness, means understanding how people view you. According to emotional intelligence expert Tasha Eurich, people who know how others see them are more skilled at showing empathy and appreciating others' views.[12] As we grow as leaders, we want to find a rich balance between the two, and one of the best ways to do this is to regularly seek critical feedback.

If you were to ask yourself the age-old existential question "Who am I as a leader?" how would you respond? How about one better: "What kind of leader do I want to become in the future?"

Ready to close the book? I don't blame you. These are hard questions, but they are the very ones we need to ask ourselves if we are to change our behaviour, because they help us grow our self-awareness.

The attributes of self-aware leaders have been well documented.[13] How do you stack up as you review this list?

- Comfortable in our own skin
- Recognize strengths, weaknesses, blind spots, and biases
- Have stores of humility
- Open to feedback
- Acknowledge we can't know everything

- Able to diagnose organizational tensions
- Strive for more than our own success

While these are a good start, they represent only half of the equation. Using the relational leadership framework, I've turbocharged each of these attributes with an extra dimension to open up our self-awareness.

- Comfortable in our own skin *and continually forming deeper relationships with others*
- Recognize strengths, weaknesses, blind spots, and biases *by finding new ways to learn and having compassion and empathy for others*
- Have stores of humility, *which helps us pay attention to how we listen and facilitate conversations to deepen understanding*
- Open to feedback, *which is absorbed and then acted upon*
- Acknowledge we can't know everything *and encourage others to develop their expertise and experience so that they can lead with confidence*
- Able to diagnose organizational tensions *and cocreate responses to complex dynamics*
- Strive for more than our own success *and consistently support others in theirs*

When we proactively embrace these attributes, we're on the road to fulfilling *both sides of the leadership equation*: the side where *we work on ourselves* and the side where *we work to develop others*. As we'll see, there is an alpha and omega in relational leadership: the more we help others, the more we help ourselves, and the more we help ourselves, the more we help others. This leads to the ultimate goal of diminished boundaries between leaders and teams.

To enhance self-awareness, it's essential to explore our leadership stories—the ones we tell ourselves and the ones we tell others. It's these stories that shape who we are as leaders. This is the reason you'll find this book filled with stories. The more you hear the stories of others, the more you are able to reflect on your own narratives. These are moments to ask yourself, *What would I do in this circumstance?* Inevitably, you will search the recesses of your experience and find a story that is roughly compatible. And in pulling it out, my hope is that you will reexamine the morals, values, and lessons it has taught you.

The challenge is that, left unstirred, these tales run silently in our unconsciousness; they not only reaffirm but actually hardwire behaviour that can set us back. They become our proof points, defensive props we summon when we feel confronted or challenged. And the stories we share with others solidify their impressions of us. They mark out boundaries in our relationships, lines not to be crossed.

As we dive into self-awareness, ask yourself whether your story has become a cloaking device or a transporter. Sometimes we hide behind our stories, using them to cast blame or portray ourselves as victims. But these same stories, told in a way that helps us learn, can change the course of our lives. For better or worse, as our experiences aggregate over time, the effects of our narratives brand us. We morph into creatures found in many a B movie. There are "victims," "schemers," "blamers," and "double agents." I worked in one place where a C-suite colleague was called the "Queen of Darkness." I'll leave it to your imagination to determine how she earned that moniker.

The deeper your "branded story" is tied to you, the more likely you are to become that character. If we're not careful, over time we can become cartoon caricatures to the people we work with. I've worked with leaders called "goose chasers," "gunslingers," "dreamers," "scatterguns," "drop-and-runs," "cowboys," and "butterfly bosses," who buzz from shiny object to shiny object. As soon as you hear yourself and others using these well-worn descriptions, it's a moment to become reflexive. It means you have been taken hostage by your own story.

A MOMENT OF TRUTH THAT CREATES A MOVEMENT

Wes Hall, chairman and founder of Kingsdale Advisors Group and founder of BlackNorth, is one of Canada's most influential businesspeople and a nationally recognized advocate for equality. He shared a story with me about the day he committed to lead a movement to end systemic racism.

On the morning of May 26, 2020, Wes woke up and prepared for another busy day ahead. It wasn't a regular Tuesday. It was the day after George Floyd was murdered in Minneapolis. Wes looked in the mirror and said to himself, "Enough is enough." He went on to explain to me that "George Floyd changed my focus. It now wasn't just about the money and making more money. Now it's about social impact and social issues."

Wes experienced what I've come to call a *moment of truth*. He smashed the mirror and replaced it with a window, helping him find new ways to think about his leadership. He resolved to take action even if he didn't know what the outcome might be. He knew what he was about to do might attract criticism, might hurt his business. But that morning, he knew that leading the way he always had wasn't enough anymore.

Wes started by publishing articles in national newspapers that invited readers to see through his eyes. He wrote about his lived experiences to help us understand the kinds of racism he and his family faced on an ongoing basis. He described, for example, answering his door at his home and the tradesman he'd hired saying to him, "Go get Mr. Hall," thinking there was no way Wes could be the one living in that elegant Rosedale home. In the very act of penning these stories, and perhaps unconsciously, Wes did what I'm going to ask you to do: he redefined his purpose and created a story reflecting his new leadership values.

After submitting the articles, Wes waited nervously for a response. The first was from Victor Dodig, CEO of one of Canada's largest banks, CIBC. Victor's words were empathetic and action oriented: the mark of a relational leader. He said, "What can I do to help?" Soon other leaders called, voicing support. The next few months of Wes's life were frenetic. He became a tireless activist and eventually founded the Canadian Council of Business Leaders Against Anti-Black Systemic Racism—also called BlackNorth. The council identifies systemic issues, starts committees to solve problems, and works with government where necessary. One of its first tasks was to track Black people in senior positions and draft targets to determine progress.

A STORY PIVOT

Wes's evolution as a leader is a remarkable story in itself. What Wes's story also shows us is the importance of collaboration. He needed the support of people across the country to make the kind of change he envisioned. Together these leaders unlocked their Rolodexes and sought out fellow leaders to embrace equity and build a genuine commitment to change. They also identified gatekeepers who might block change: "Those gatekeepers who fail to act must be moved aside."[14] They *cocreated* the BlackNorth pledge, which would commit leaders to advance and measure their initiatives. They convened a series of summits, and as of today more than five hundred organizations have signed on.

The 8 minutes and 46 seconds that ended George Floyd's life profoundly affected the world. While protests were held in more than sixty countries, how many of them produced what Wes Hall was able to as a result of saying to himself, "Enough is enough"? Wes posed the question as much to himself as he did to us: "What does a future with new possibilities look like?" In our interview he shared his new mantra: "We need permanent change." Wes not only embodies the new spirit of leadership but has shown us how a new level of self-awareness has changed his life—and has impacted the lives of many others as a result.

REFLEXIVITY

Wes's story demonstrates how self-awareness can grow when we use the first relational practice: reflexivity. This is the first practice I developed to help people get in touch with their inner leader. I came to call this practice the "new yoga of leadership." It teaches you to *bend back* on yourself to see where you have come from, *centre yourself* to define where you presently stand, and *lunge ahead* to determine where you need to go. This practice forces us to question assumptions, and in so doing, reveals our blind spots.

While there are many experts in self-awareness, I was drawn to the pioneering work of Ann Cunliffe, a professor of organization studies, because of the way she defines this core element of self-awareness.[15]

Simply put, reflexivity is a way to critically question past actions to see future possibilities. Harnessing reflexivity means *engaging* in rich, deep observation. This means developing observational skills to acknowledge, analyze, understand, and recall our surroundings and the elements within them. Disciplining yourself to see in rich detail better prepares you to address workplace predicaments. You'll also become more adept at solving problems because you'll be identifying the source of issues and making logical connections between them.

Reflexivity is the true definition of how we become more transparent and authentic. For many leaders, it's not a question of wanting to change, it's knowing *how* to change. And this is where reflexivity becomes our teacher. The secret lies in using this practice to analyze your past to put the wheels in motion for a more self-informed future. The ultimate reflexive question is, "What will I do differently . . . next time?"

A reflexive stance grows your ability to expose and tease out the complexities of authority and power relations in our world. It's a gift, not a grilling, allowing us to create new stories that help us replace bad behaviours that may be holding us back. But beware, the longer you allow old stories to play in your head, the more fixed and harder to dislodge they become. The discipline of reflexivity helps us continually refresh and renew the stories we tell ourselves.

Reflexivity demands you become highly self-critical. You need to find the place where you are at a fault, face up to it, and then do something about it. An uneasiness in the pit of your stomach is usually the sign that you're due for a reflexive check-in. Explore your actions by recalling the incident with as much vivid detail as you can—not easy work, especially if you've been rocked and hurt by it. "Talk it out" by creating a video where you unpack what happened. The hard work is then watching that video and pinpointing where you might have let yourself (and likely others) down. "Write it out" by pouring your thoughts out to your journal. Reread what you've written to find the clues of where you need to change. "Think it through" by working with a coach or talking to a close friend. Whatever method you choose, don't look away.

Think back to the kinds of emotions you displayed. Think hard about how others reacted to you. These are the moments that reveal blind spots, unconscious thinking, assumptions, and the things we take for granted. That's what you're looking for. These pernicious behaviours are the key to processing how our actions contributed to a situation. From there, examine the intended—and unintended—consequences of your actions. Next comes the heavy lifting of deciding what you need to do to rectify the situation and/or make amends. This may mean getting more training in a certain area or apologizing to a coworker—whatever course of action you determine, stick with it, and see it through. You'll know your *reflexive skill* is improving when you feel more comfortable and less defensive about receiving feedback. You'll know you've made the *reflexive turn* when you finally feel at peace with the situation. When you hear the self-talk in your head saying "Wow, I won't ever do that again! Here's what I will do . . . ," you're on your way.

The benefit of being reflexive is that we begin to know ourselves for who we truly are; with this insight, we are able to identify and adjust behaviours that negatively impact others. Knowing the impact that our personality has on our workplace is the first step in the relational framework, the foundation that takes us to the next steps of becoming more compassionate, empowering others, and fostering a stronger culture.

HOW YOUR BEHAVIOURS CAN SABOTAGE YOU

While participating in a Zoom meeting with a selection committee to choose their next president, I learned how important self-awareness is. We were talking about the traps of unconscious bias in hiring, and as we went around the virtual table introducing ourselves, a member of the committee, a white male we'll call "Javier," said, "At least you don't have to worry about me. I have no bias."

But I *was* worried about Javier. I wondered how many missteps he might have already made that had hurt him—and his organization—without even knowing it. Seeing the collective eyebrows raised on Zoom spoke volumes. It's people like Javier who think they're not biased that need to develop greater self-awareness.

The problem for leaders like Javier is recognizing how their behaviours may sabotage their efforts. As we saw in his remark, lack of self-awareness often shows up in the form of automatic defensiveness. But there are other clues to watch out for. Sudden anxiety or jangly nerves. Erratic emotions. Explanations that aren't called for. Alternate views that get shut down. Tempers flare. Guts churn. Patience runs out. A headache develops. Listening stops. A light sweat breaks out. Anytime we see these symptoms in ourselves—or witness them in others—it's a sign, a call to action to become more self-aware.

IDENTIFYING THE MOMENTS OF TRUTH THAT LEAD TO SELF-AWARENESS

There are times in all of our lives that we might describe as no-turning-back moments of change. Moments that are unreconciled. Times when we know we must move forward *even if* we don't know what the consequences will be. Our character, resilience, and resolve are tested in ways that we probably haven't ever experienced. The gravity of the moment produces all kinds of physical, emotional, and psychological reactions. We likely feel unhinged, out of control, and lost. It's in these moments that we need a practice that will help us process what's going on around us. A way to see that there is a light at the end of the tunnel. You will have likely already had, or will have, many experiences that have changed your life. The question is, How did you recover? How did you benefit from them? What lessons did you learn? How did you take what you learned to help others? More significantly, have you made peace with the moment and are you able to move on? By responding to these questions, you are awakening your self-awareness.

A moment of truth should have the potential to uplift your heart, mind, and soul. But most importantly, it's a moment that stops you in your tracks. It should be a moment that holds the promise of both professional and personal transformation. To identify these pivotal moments, be on the lookout for experiences and incidents that affect you deeply in the following six ways.

- **A shock to the system:** These moments take the form of a profound crisis (as Wes Hall's moment of truth was). You might lose a loved one, get a divorce, get fired. Perhaps you were working on a big project that went off the rails and you failed miserably. These cataclysmic experiences need to be harnessed, not buried. We need to learn from both our experience and our mistakes.

- **Regret and/or remorse:** These are times when we are in the midst of ethical dilemmas. We might have misread a situation and made incorrect assumptions. When we look back, we may have contributed to and/or enabled toxicity. We may have feelings of guilt or shame; we likely beat ourselves up. But we need to do more than that. Moments of regret are an opening to explore our inner beliefs and analyze our actions.

- **Receiving hard feedback and/or advice that causes us to question ourselves:** These moments occur when someone sits us down and shares their views on our behaviour or response to a situation. Don't be the leader who shrugs off this advice. Take it in, digest it, and use it as a valuable tool to help you change.

- **Positive and negative role models:** We all know that a bad boss can make us an even worse boss. Poor leadership makes us jaded and untrusting of colleagues and of ourselves. We need to treat these moments of adversity for what they are: windows of opportunity to ensure that we will never act that way. As an experienced leader once told me, "I see the behaviour I like in a leader and use it. But I make a point to leave the ugly stuff behind."

- **Blinding flashes of the obvious:** All of us wish we had a PhD in hindsight. These moments occur when at long last we have an epiphany or aha moment. It can be frustrating not to get to the answer quickly, but these moments tend to pop up when we've given ourselves distance from challenges and return to them with fresh eyes.

- **Standing up for what we believe in:** What's your red line in the sand? It's in these moments of truth that we distinguish ourselves; we are not afraid to stand up for what we

believe in. These may be some of the most conflicted moments in our careers. This is where having your purpose
story puts you on firm ground.

Let's face it: no one likes to be uncomfortable, and that's what a
moment of truth is. It's much easier to stare down the shortcomings of
others than to do it for ourselves. And this is probably why we largely
ignore the times when we've failed or caved. Maintaining the status
quo is certainly much easier.

As I spoke with leaders about moments of truth that changed how
they thought of themselves as leaders, here are a few of the stories they
shared:

> Without a doubt, if you want to talk about the mo-
> ment that shaped my leadership, it was the moment
> when my uncle came to visit from California after my
> father's funeral. He came up for the funeral, my moth-
> er's brother. He was mythical. We'd never met. He was
> this big man. And you know, Uncle Bob said, "You're
> the man of the house now, you have to look after your
> mom." . . . I was upset when my father died but I wasn't
> scared. It was like, okay, I got this. I can do this. From
> then on, I was very independent. I never went past
> high school. I had teachers fail me, not because of my
> test scores. They couldn't believe I could get these test
> scores without showing up.
> —*Jake Gold, CEO, The Management Trust*

Shocks to the system are moments of truth that profoundly alter
the course of lives. Jake was seventeen at the time of his father's passing
and was thrust into a role to help support his grieving mom, brothers,
and sisters. We see him managing his emotions as he's upset but "not
scared," and with that came a quiet confidence that he could do this.
The moment heightened Jake's entrepreneurial spirit as he saw how
easily he could absorb information from school without attending.
From this pivotal moment, we can see how Jake's leadership evolved as

he went on to manage the band The Tragically Hip and found his own talent management company, The Management Trust.

> We actually had a meeting and said, "Should we go bankrupt?" We said, "Hell no, we have something here!"
> —*Michael Hirsh, CEO, WOW! Unlimited Media*

In this blinding flash of the obvious, we see Michael Hirsh, a pioneer in digital animation, work through one of the most challenging times of his then-young career. He had formed a small company, Nelvana, with partners Clive Smith and Patrick Loubert, in the 1970s. The company had grown exponentially, morphing from one hundred to four hundred people based on how busy they were. The challenges of filling the sales pipeline, hiring the best, building up infrastructure, and developing more sophisticated accounting and legal systems all collided at a time when interest rates were hovering at 20%. The company was about to go under.

It was in this moment that things crystallized for Michael. One of the first things he realized was that each partner had a particular strength. Clive was an animator, Patrick excelled at production. And Michael excelled in sales and strategic growth. The moment of truth spurred each of these three leaders to dig down and not only embrace their unique strengths but turbocharge them. In Michael's case, the crisis compelled him to "really lead" by selling hundreds of hours of programming. And by doing this, the company was able to earn enough money to pay down its debt. You can't help but wonder how much that moment in the '70s contributed to the moment in 2000 when Nelvana was acquired by Corus for a cool $540 million.[16]

> I think this is true of a lot of people put into new leadership positions. I was successful in my old jobs, and so I should be successful in this job. No problem. I had no idea what I was getting into. I also inherited, I'm sure like every leader says, I inherited some psychopaths. There were two guys in senior positions, and they'd

been talking to them for years, but it was a complete
failure of leadership . . . But I waited [to fire them]. If I
had to do it over again, I would have fired them sooner.
                    —*Jonathan Kay, editor,* Quillette

Many leaders have heard the maxim "Hire slow, fire fast," and
so Jonathan Kay's regret at not firing faster will be no surprise. But
it's Jonathan's self-revelation that the leadership skills he honed at
the *National Post*, a daily newspaper, would not carry the day at *The
Walrus*, a monthly national magazine, that shows us how important
it is to get a lay of the land when we take on new roles or new assignments. In Jonathan's example and the next, we see how important it is
for leaders to question another maxim: experience is the best teacher.

I lost out. I had built the department of stakeholder
relations. I was de facto VP for about five months. Of
course, I threw my hat in the ring. And I competed really hard to get the VP position. I lost it to an outsider.
But I had a member of the board who supported me.
And he said, "Okay, well, fine. She's not getting the job,
but I want her to have leadership training."
                    —*Wendy Zatylny*

In Wendy Zatylny's moment of truth we feel the pain of her loss, of
working so hard to compete for a role and not being successful. Many
leaders struggle after such a loss; they may lose confidence, become
bitter, and begin "mailing it in." Not Wendy. She relied on her inner
strength to get through her crisis and renew her commitment to the
company. Bad shit is going to happen to all of us. It's just a matter of
time. We can gripe about it . . . or . . . we can ask for help. Getting the
resources you need will help you dig down deep and keep going. It's
worth noting that a big part of Wendy's ability to pull herself up was
that she had an advocate who supported her through this tough moment. When you find yourself in a similar situation, remember to not
just ask for help, but ask, "Who can help?" Wendy's hard work paid off;
she was the CEO of the Association of Canadian Port Authorities for

nine years and is now leading the Canadian operations of a leading wireless communications organization.

IDENTIFYING MOMENTS OF TRUTH

As you reflect on the stories above, make a mental note about what makes these experiences moments of truth. The first thing to notice is that these stories have staying power. When I asked leaders to reflect on what changed them or affected them deeply, it took them mere seconds to remember. Old pain, remorse, and regret may fade over time, but they never really leave us. This is why it's so helpful to have a practice you can use in the moment; left unattended, unresolved events can destroy confidence—or worse, fester into bitterness. As we've said, this isn't work for fainthearted leaders. These moments reveal how we judge and what we judge; they explore why we place higher or lower value on people, ideas, causes, and events. They create discomfort, exposing how we see ourselves, which is often in stark contrast to how others see us.

And while acknowledging these moments sparks self-awareness, that's not enough. Once we've realized that our behaviour has created harm, we need to jump into action, adjusting our behaviour along the way. As you read the stories coming up, be on the lookout for the crucible of the moment. These are the tipping points that cause people to change. Coaches often talk about these as "teachable moments." It could be as subtle as the look on someone's face that shows you you've hurt them, or as dramatic as your accountant telling you to call the insolvency experts. In these moments you are literally teaching yourself to change. When the penny finally drops, everything seems so clear. You say to yourself, "Now I get it" or "I never thought about it that way"—just like Wes Hall did. You typically join the "never again club," vowing to *stop a behaviour* and *start* a new one. A helpful next step is to come up with a motto or mantra, reminding yourself to keep the promises you made to yourself. Finally, for a moment of truth to "count," you'll want to identify a series of action steps that makes the transformation real.

This practice is designed to help you not only identify but *meet the moment* in ways that build self-awareness. What we've seen in these stories and those that follow is that it's only when we face up to what we find downright uncomfortable that we are able to change. It's in these moments that your true self appears: the assumptions you hold, blind spots that haunt you, and all the things you take for granted. It's only in confronting these demons that real change can happen.

HAD IT ALL BUT STILL UNHAPPY

Kunal Gupta built his company, Nova (formerly called Polar), during the tail end of his undergraduate degree. With outposts in Toronto, New York, London, and Sydney, Nova's clients include hundreds of media agencies publishing in thirty countries. Given the size and complexity of his organization, you can imagine my surprise when I heard that Kunal only works about five or six hours a day. Inwardly, I had to ask myself, *What have I been doing wrong all these years?*

> Kunal: I'm at the top for six years—but I didn't feel any different. I thought if I got to the top, all of these things would start to happen. I started to turn inwards. It really helped me to see myself and others. A light turned on. I began with deep questioning, asking myself, "What do I value? What do I believe?" I had inherited all these beliefs. The process of looking inward helped me to face long-held values and beliefs that might have been holding me back. It was this moment that ignited my transformation.
>
> Jill: How did you change?
>
> Kunal: I became more aware of myself—and others; I became more empathetic. In the old days if I lost a piece of business, I would put a lot of pressure on myself—eeeecccchhhhh! In this next phase of my leadership, I still might lose a piece of business, but I don't react in the same way. Everything has changed,

> I've moved from seeing things from a one-dimensional
> to a four-dimensional stance.

Kunal said that before he began to focus internally, he had a "victim" mindset. He went on to say that once he accepted change as a permanent given, this new mindset allowed him to "think forward," a way to not dwell on the present minutiae that might have been holding him back. In this case, the moment arrived when he recognized—and accepted—that a different pace of change had taken hold, one that he had not yet become accustomed to and that he could not control. With this reflection, Kunal shared with me his new mantra: "I don't meet change with resistance."

Kunal said that one day, after working fiendishly for years, he experienced a moment similar to Wes Hall's, during which he wondered, "Is that all there is?" He had arrived at the pinnacle of success, and yet . . . he wasn't as happy as he thought he would be when the moment came. He found his way back by turning inward and developing discipline through yoga and meditation. He became aware of his thoughts and resisted the urge to control them. He accepted whatever came into his awareness and always remained alert. And he got into action. Once the pandemic was over, he moved to Portugal without knowing a soul. He learned Portuguese, developed a new circle of friends, and empowered his team to continue to grow the business. About a year later, I was intrigued to read in his blog that he made the decision to no longer be "founder-led and founder-run" or identified solely by the company he had built. Kunal had experienced another moment of truth and shared a new level of self-awareness: "If my identity were visualized as a pie chart, when I started the business 15 years ago, the pie would probably have only one big slice. My business was my identity. . . . Over time, the pie has grown, and new slices have been added."[17]

HAD IT ALL AND LOST IT

Guess what? People in the art world talk. Reputations and careers can be made or destroyed by an air kiss at a cocktail party. Imagine having one of your first art galleries fold in that kind of environment. Jamie Angell is a veteran of the art scene, having opened his first art gallery in 1996, and has seen many gallery owners—and artists—come and go.

Jamie recently celebrated the twenty-fifth anniversary of the Angell Gallery. When I met with Jamie, he shared with me that he'd started out as a hairdresser to some of Toronto's top celebrities. As a result, he became a great listener and developed an ease with well-heeled clients. Along the way, he became enthralled with the Yorkville art scene and opened his own gallery. He survived the early years in his gallery by cutting hair in the back. And then one day, he realized that he would have to close the gallery. Devastated by this moment of truth, he told me what happened next:

> After the gallery closed, I remember I leapt out of bed, I went to my back patio and started writing in my journal and then I bawled my eyes out. And the epiphany I had was that you could say whatever you want, but you can't take my purpose, my passion away from me. That was a huge turning point. So ever since that point, I stopped caring a lot less, not all together, but a lot less about what people said. It's that purpose that drives me.
>
> —*Jamie Angell, founder, Angell Gallery*

No one would have blamed Jamie if he'd stayed in bed after his first gallery shuttered. But somewhere deep inside, he found the strength to confront the loss and figure out what he would do better the next time around.

Jamie's story shows us how vital it is to work with our emotions rather than burying or fighting them. Only by processing what's happened are we able to move forward. Jamie is a leader with tremendous resolve and grit, and he is not afraid to stand tall and share his mantra: "No one can take my purpose, my passion away from me."

BECOMING COMFORTABLE WITH BEING UNCOMFORTABLE

In 1995 when Diane Brisebois assumed the role of CEO at Retail Council of Canada, it was a sixty-year-old organization—and industry—dominated by men. I should know. I worked there for four years before she arrived, left, and then came back as an SVP of strategic initiatives to support her vision. You can imagine the stir that this appointment caused in retail circles at a time when terms like *unconscious bias*, *gender equity*, and *#metoo* were still decades away.

When I had the pleasure of meeting back up with Diane, she shared a moment of truth that happened early in her tenure and was seminal in her development as leader of this national trade association:

> One of the biggest lessons as a leader is not to take things for granted—there is always a lesson to be learned. Decades ago, I was a main-stage speaker at a hard goods industry conference. There were more than eight hundred people, mostly men. I walked in through a side door and sat down, and I heard men behind me commenting on my presence—without knowing I was the speaker about to take the stage.
>
> Then one of the senior gentlemen from the conference—who also didn't know who I was—sat next to me and asked, "Do you know where the coffee is?" He then just looked at me, expecting me not only to know where the coffee was but also to get him a cup. About fifteen minutes later, I was introduced as the keynote speaker—and as I took the stage, I looked back to where I had been seated and could see their shock and embarrassment.
>
> I could have chosen several paths at that point in time. One would have been to try to prove that I was worthy of being on stage as one of the few women in the room. The other one, which I chose, was to realize that *I deserved* to be on stage—to use my knowledge and my presence on that stage to break barriers, to set a positive example, and to turn the moment into

a great learning experience. I knew that I was forcing many of the men in the room out of their comfort zone—I wasn't resentful, I was elated!

Over the years, as I became more established and more acknowledged as a leader, I replayed that and many more of those very awkward experiences in my mind. I did so to remind myself and others, especially those who were trying to break barriers, that we all deserve to be on stage. I spend quite a bit of time sharing these experiences with those leading teams and those who aspire to lead. Our teams include men and women, visible minorities, and people with disabilities—and they are all precious. As leaders, we have a marvelous opportunity to give them strength, confidence, and hope.

We do all deserve to be on stage!

—*Diane J. Brisebois, president and CEO,*
Retail Council of Canada

What would you have done if you were Diane? It would be tempting to call out those men, wouldn't it? But something kicked in as Diane sat in that darkened hall, getting ready to take the stage. Everything that had made her the leader she was up until that moment fused; in her internal dialogue we see how she was teaching herself in the moment, aspiring to become a higher-purpose leader that day.

This is a good example of how a leader uses reflexivity to see things from different angles. We see Diane sizing up the situation, deeply observing the behaviours of the men around her. We also see her exposing the subtleties and nuance of the moment as she evaluates the power games going on around her. We witness Diane's self-revelation about how this moment could define how the industry might view her in the future and that by taking the high road she gained new inner strength to be comfortable in her leadership.

STANDING STRONG IN THE FACE OF ADVERSITY

One of the biggest moments of truth for a leader is taking on a new job. Successful leaders are continually fending off calls from headhunters urging them to make that next big move. But how do you know that move is going to be the right one? Gaëtane Verna's decision to move from a small town in Quebec to take on the leadership of an art gallery in Toronto could have proved her undoing. But in her story, we see moments of truth that increased her self-awareness, built her confidence, and provided her with the experience to take on a bold new leadership role in the US.

Imagine the hard knocks of arriving in a new city, where you are largely unknown, to take on the leadership of a contemporary art gallery. Gaëtane had enjoyed success as executive director and chief curator of the Musée d'art de Joliette in Quebec but quickly felt undercurrents all around her that almost pulled her under. When she came to Toronto in 2012 to become executive director of The Power Plant, an art gallery in what had been an actual power plant until 1980, she faced an uphill battle competing with the likes of the Art Gallery of Ontario and the Royal Ontario Museum. Remembering those early days, she said, "We don't have any Lawren Harris paintings here, we don't have dinosaurs. I would say, we were at the bottom of the pole." She needed to find a new way to position The Power Plant as a vibrant alternative to these established institutions.

Gaëtane's moment of truth occurred when she resolved not to turn back. She had to leave behind the comfortable world she knew and navigate one filled with complex hierarchies of power, politics, and racism. While her story centres on the art world, it's one that continues to play out in organizations everywhere, where microaggressions and assumptions continue to hold back women as well as racialized and marginalized people. She shared her early memories of her "welcome" to Toronto:

> I'm in this new role in Ontario, Francophone, Black, you know Haitian, not from the Guggenheim, not anything sexy. I didn't realize the pressure of the job. But like in every place in the world, good people quietly

stand by you. People were coming to me and saying, "I know you're having a hard time but I'm supporting you." I think there are different kinds of people in this world. There are people who recognize quality and make decisions independently. They support you when you are at your lowest. Then there's people who wait until you show them you've got the chops.

—Gaëtane Verna, executive director,
Wexner Center for the Arts at Ohio State

Once she had come to terms and made the decision to move, Gaëtane got to work. While she knew many artists, she realized these relationships weren't enough. So she moved out of her comfort zone and got to know Toronto's donors, influencers, and leading organizations. In the face of adversity, she was fortunate to have the encouragement of a strong chair, a supportive family, and a small group of key mentors who urged her to keep going.

Another moment of truth came serendipitously. When she was at a low point, Gaëtane found inner strength by holding on to a piece of advice she received from artist and photographer Arnaud Maggs. He told her, "In life you have to work hard even if you think no one is watching." She told me she never forgot that. This became her mantra. It helped her to become a chameleon, developing new behaviours to meet each new moment she encountered.

Being asked to speak at events was also a moment of truth. Even if you feel nervous about public speaking, seek out platforms to share leadership experience. The simple act of preparing remarks is a great way to grow self-awareness, compelling you to reflect on your story and how it's changing. When Gaëtane opened the first meeting of the Black Curators Forum in the fall of 2019, she shared: "Each time I acknowledge the land that our gallery stands on, I think about erasure— of people and of stories. I think about those who have the privilege of writing history and about the people they choose, sometimes violently, to ignore. I think about the many trailblazers who paved the way for us to be here tonight but whose stories are largely untold." By sharing her commitment to bring these stories to life, she became a trailblazer in her own right.

Fast-forward to 2022, and Gaëtane's commitment to master her moments of truth has paid off. After producing new programs, touring successful shows nationally, and finding additional sources of revenue to increase The Power Plant's budget by more than 50%, she was invited to lead the prestigious Wexner Center for the Arts in Ohio.[18]

SELF-DEVELOPMENT BUILDS SELF-AWARENESS

> Is the thing that I wanted ten years ago still the thing I want? I began to broaden my network and talk to people who have different or adjacent careers. I started talking to the next generation. Looking at them, their expectations around work and how they were demanding their workplaces support their continual growth and careers. At first, I thought how fucking entitled, but then later, I began thinking, no, good for them. And then I was like, why didn't I do that? My generation, Generation X, we are the translators between the boomers and Generation Z. It feels strangely selfish or disloyal to the company, but I'm living these values, plotting my way, and staying in a role long enough to learn what I need.
>
> —*Adria Miller, director, development, major and principal gifts, University of Toronto*

In Adria's questioning of where her future lies, she consciously compares herself to the behaviours of the new generation coming up behind her. In seeing how much help the next generation received, she realized she, too, needs support. By observing what's going on around her, she was able to shape and inform what she needed to be a good leader. But in order to get there, there are emotional triggers ("how fucking entitled") that Adria needed to explore. Instead of being angry about why others are getting more help than she did, she developed a mindset that asked, "Why am I not getting the help I need?"

Like many in her generation, Adria had a number of quick, successive jobs with growing responsibilities. And while she learned a lot along the way, she didn't feel she was given as much opportunity to grow through mentoring and more formalized learning opportunities. Clearly it was Adria's fast learning through adjacent careers that helped get her to the point she is today. The question she's asking now is, Will it be enough to get her that next big promotion?

Adria's choice to cast herself as "translator" between boomers and Generation Z is another moment of awakening as she sees a role for herself to develop stronger communication and act as a connector between generations, helping them find common ground. As Adria described this role, it made me wonder how many organizations have squandered opportunities like this to better serve the needs and interests of multiple generations working together. Her new vocation of becoming that bridge between generations is an example of using newfound confidence to take action.

THE IMPORTANCE OF REFLEXIVITY

Kunal, Jamie, Diane, Gaëtane, and Adria's stories illustrate how reflexivity can help you when you face your next serious challenge or crisis. We saw in their stories how they "bent back on themselves" to renew their passion and purpose. Each one questioned their innermost beliefs, finding new ways to think and behave.

In Kunal's story we learned that in order to grow, he had to redefine the core values of what it meant for him to be "successful" and "on top of the world." He became a calmer person as a result of it, accepting that he couldn't win every piece of business—a hard thing for any successful entrepreneur to swallow. In his moment of truth, we saw him pivot from his external view of success (winning more business) to an internal view that helped him become more reflective and purpose driven.

In Jamie's story we saw a leader build resolve not to give up. "Writing it out," Jamie took pen to paper, reigniting his passion and commitment to contemporary art, and spurred himself on to develop plans for his next gallery. In his story we see how important it is to look in the mirror, much like Wes did, to create for himself a *new* story.

Diane's story highlights an important element of reflexive practice: recognizing that when you are uncomfortable, it is actually a gift to see things in a new light. Diane asserts a quiet confidence, realizing she doesn't always need to "prove" herself. That moment also taught Diane a lesson that she now uses to coach her team: encouraging them to take more time to listen to others and appreciate their lived experience.

In Gaëtane's moment of truth we see a leader who met adversity with resilience. Her calling card was that she was in constant action—learning about the new city she moved to, developing new relationships, forging partnerships, identifying mutual interests with sponsors that grew revenue. With the support of allies who believed in her, she was able to "talk it through" and received the counsel she needed. She was able to achieve these feats in part because she stuck to her mantra. Even though she might not have felt that anyone was watching her, in fact they were! What's your mantra? How has it changed over the years? Think about how your mantra might change as you work through the seven practices to develop your self-awareness.

Adria's experience reveals a growing awareness of what it will take for her to reach the next level in her career. She not only appreciates this but acts on it, developing her network and learning from the generation coming up after her. We also see a leader who is ready, willing, and able to take on the vital role of translator between generations: a capability that will be in high demand in the coming years as workplaces continue to grapple with multiple perspectives and views on authority.

Self-awareness is so much more than knowing ourselves—it's about knowing and appreciating others. When we make that quantum leap to move from ourselves to learn about others' lived experiences, we have a much better vantage point to see ourselves through their eyes.

PRACTICE BECOMING MORE SELF-AWARE

Here are the seven steps I've developed to grow your self-awareness:

- **Step 1: Look back to look ahead.** Identify an experience that you would describe as a *moment of truth*. Listen to your inner voice. If it's telling you, "Something's not right here," you're onto something. You'll know you have the right story when you remember it like it was yesterday, when you felt particularly uncomfortable, or when you felt intense moments of doubt about your actions and their consequences.

- **Step 2: Unpack your story.** Bend back on yourself to see who you truly are. Recall the story in as much vivid detail as you can. Take responsibility by asking yourself, "What role did I play in all this?" rather than looking to blame others or find excuses for your actions. This could be through writing the story down, videoing yourself telling the story, or getting together with a trusted friend and telling them the story. Explore what's been revealed.

- **Step 3: Use "what" and "how" reflexive questions (rather than "why") to change behaviour.**
  - What was the trigger that made me act the way I did? (Did I want to win at all costs? Was I fearful? In denial? Did I think I knew better than everyone else?)
  - What patterns of my behaviour were revealed?
  - How did I portray myself? Identify where you might have been hiding from the truth (for example, places where you cast yourself as a victim or an ingenue).
  - How did blind spots and/or assumptions prevent me from seeing clearly?
  - How have my actions hurt others? Have I made amends?
  - What stopped me from being able to see possible outcomes of my actions?
  - What would I do differently if I could do it over again?

- **Step 4: Develop a 360 view.** Should you have included more people to inform your actions? Done more research?

Reached out to a mentor? The trick here is to toggle between building internal and external self-awareness. Begin by focusing internally to reveal your values and motivations. Next, pivot externally. Ask those around you—your boss, peers, those who report to you—about how they viewed the event. Ask them how your actions affected them. It takes courage to do this, and you might not like what you hear. But understanding our impact on others helps us to change.

- **Step 5: Own it.** Building self-awareness begins with listening to the voice inside your head: the one you may be ignoring. You may feel depressed, confused, hurt, or all three. There will be days you want to run from it. Don't. Commit to deep reflection, and journal at least once a week. It doesn't take a lot of time, and as you look back, it gives you a handy reference point to track your progress.

- **Step 6: Start an advisory board to ensure regular feedback.** Identify colleagues whose opinions and expertise you value and trust. Ask them to support your leadership by being a lifeline when you encounter challenging moments. Just knowing that support is there will make you feel calmer and more centred.

- **Step 7: Get into action.** Crystallize your purpose and passion. Document what you've learned about yourself, and develop a never-stop-learning mindset. Now here comes the magic moment: time to exercise that reflexive muscle. Try out your new behaviours in upcoming conversations and meetings. Make notes about what worked well—and not so well. Adapt your behaviour as you encounter different circumstances. Be the chameleon. This is where reflexivity can help, as it compels you to step back and check for faulty assumptions. Be proactive in seeking feedback from peers, friends, and family, and embed these insights into your leadership. Keep practicing this continual cycle of trying out new things, documenting reactions, and receiving feedback, and you'll soon have all of the marks of a self-aware relational leader.

ON A PRACTICAL NOTE—DEVELOP YOUR PURPOSE STORY

It is hard and ongoing work to build self-awareness, practice reflexivity, and develop your purpose story. As a busy leader with many demands on your time, one of the biggest challenges may be how to find the time to do this work. It's one thing in theory to want to reflect, grow, and evolve as a leader; quite another to make it part of your busy week. A few suggestions: Make a meeting with yourself each week; take it off-site so that you won't be distracted. Connect with a peer group and book time together to meet and share experiences. Take time to get away from your computer altogether. Go for a walk. Join others for coffee and conversation. Take a break from to-do lists and make a to-dream list. Jot down insights, capture your thoughts and feelings. In this way you'll start to mark your progress.

Throughout this chapter, we talked about the need for leaders to develop their purpose story. To help you get moving, get out your journal or open a document on your laptop. Think about the stories you've read, the leader you are, and the leader you wish to become. Reflect deeply on what's brought you to this place today.

Once you've captured your thoughts, answer these questions:

- Who am I?
- What do I do?
- Who do I do it for?
- What do these people want or need?
- How do they change as a result?
- How do I relate with others?
- What are the principles and values that define me?
- How have I grown?
- What might be stopping me from changing?
- How do I wish to lead in the future?

They are lifelong questions. These questions create a starting point for your story. Make a plan to revisit your story at least once a year. I usually like to review mine at the end of each year. You'll be surprised by how much you've changed. Once you've reviewed it, make a new one and keep the process going. With enough practice you'll soon see yourself as a leader who is at once relational, digital, and disruptive. Just the kind of leader that the 2020s demand.

Evaluate Your Performance

As you think about your degree of self-awareness, ask yourself these questions:

- When you look back, what moment of truth changed your life?

  _____

  _____

  _____

- How did this moment affect you?

  _____

  _____

  _____

- What is the story you tell yourself when you think of this moment?

  _____

  _____

  _____

- How has the story changed over time?

  _____

  _____

  _____

- What mantra emerged?

  _____

  _____

  _____

- What is the moral of your story?

  _____

  _____

  _____

- What leadership behaviour stands out as the one you would most like to improve upon?

  _____

  _____

  _____

- What experiences should you actively seek out to change this behaviour?

  _____

  _____

  _____

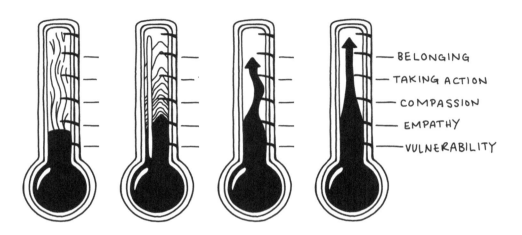

CHAPTER 3

BELONGING
TAKING ACTION
COMPASSION
EMPATHY
VULNERABILITY

Practice Compassion

Compassion is not about singing kumbaya. It's more than just showing warmth—it takes competence too.[19]
—Adam Grant, professor

COMPASSION IS EMPATHY IN ACTION

One cold weekend in January 2022, I found myself immersed in the NFL Wild Card Weekend, watching teams duke it out for the privilege of advancing to the divisional round. Part of my interest was to see how teams compared to my beloved Buffalo Bills, but another part of it was to kill time as Toronto was in yet another COVID lockdown.

The game between the Tampa Bay Buccaneers and Philadelphia Eagles caught my attention. During the third quarter the Eagles fumbled a punt return, and the Buccaneers' defensive back Andrew Adams went into the melee to pull Eagles out of the pile. In response,

Coach Bruce Arians smacked him in the head. I looked at my husband, Gordon, and said, "Did that really just happen?" Numerous slow-motion replays left no doubt. A pile of players from both teams fought for the ball, which the Bucs eventually recovered. Arians was upset because pulling an opponent from a pile during a scrum can draw a penalty. The coach followed up for good measure with an elbow to Adams's shoulder. Arians said he was trying to "help" Adams from drawing a penalty.

Arians's aggression, coupled with an outcry on social media, prompted a second look. By midweek the NFL had fined him $50,000 for this poor behaviour. "I'll appeal it," Arians told reporters. "It ain't got nothing to do with the game, so we're good."[20]

Actually, we're not good. And how we treat people has everything to do with the game.

This may be a dramatic example, but it's a telling one, and the fall-out can be severe. Public relations disasters, the real and perceived value of your organization, loss of employees, lost prestige—all these challenges surface with misguided actions and words. This same scenario plays out daily in businesses where leaders have become disconnected from the reality of how leadership has evolved and what employees expect. Just because you may have the title of coach or CEO, the old ways of enforcing leadership from above won't get you very far these days. When leaders work autonomously, using old-style command and control like Coach Arians did, things rarely turn out well. This style of leadership makes people feel intimidated, unsafe, not included, and not heard. They become timid about voicing their views or opinions and ultimately withdraw. Which benefits no one.

This is why practice two—becoming a more compassionate leader—is so vital. Growing compassion helps leaders better appreciate the lived experiences of others and, most significantly, empowers them to engage. It's a whole new way to think about how we define what it means to "lead" and what it means to "follow."

THE BASICS OF COMPASSION

Socrates said that when we know someone else, we know ourselves better. This knowledge, in turn, is reinforcing, helping us to better appreciate and value others. The stories you will read in practice two demonstrate that in order to become more compassionate, we must first make the shift from *self-fulness* to *selflessness*.

We hear many leaders speak today about the importance of putting themselves in someone else's shoes. While feeling for others is admirable, it's not enough. Compassion means cosuffering: so much so that the leader feels compelled to do something about it. But stop: When someone tells you a story about their troubles, do you leap in and tell them a story of your own misfortunes? Don't fall victim to getting into "story wars," where your tale is more dramatic and diminishes theirs.

When someone has gotten up the courage to share their story, stop everything, put your phone down, lock eyes with them, and really listen to what they are telling you. Assess how deeply the person is injured; they might need counselling support or therapy. As a leader, you want to make sure you have a list of resources available to support team members. If the person is ready and open to it, ask questions that will help them see possible ways forward—that all is not lost. You may have some ideas of your own. The main thing is to help them take even the tiniest of first steps.

A McKinsey study identified four behaviours to help leaders become more compassionate: awareness of context, vulnerability, empathy, and an ability to make people feel cared for.[21] Combined, these behaviours help us become a proactive advocate for others. As we become more mindful of the hopes, needs, concerns, insights, and aspirations of others, they, too, will become more compassionate. Running side by side with others is a much different exercise than cheering them on from the stands. This is the intimate space of compassion. It's here where others' feelings are validated, their life experiences honoured and respected. And it's here where they feel accepted and connected to the whole.

But what does that look like in the real world?

An example of compassion was in full view with health care workers during the pandemic. We saw examples from around the world where health care professionals practiced relational behaviours—having their antennae up, trading stories, and sharing advice on what was working, what to expect, and what surprises to look out for. Doctors, nurses, and personal support workers alike *showed each other compassion* so that they could be fully present to aid their patients. In the highly stratified world of hospitals, staff at every level were sharing in the experience and supporting each other as human beings.

Another example is a story that was shared with me by a CEO whose second-in-command I was coaching. The CEO was relatively new in the job, and like many new leaders, had to make sweeping changes to the organization. Many people were terminated; financial cuts took their toll on culture. As tough as they were, those decisions needed to be made. There was a moment in our conversation that struck me about the power of the *compassion advantage*. The CEO shared that after all the stress *they* had endured, the second-in-command came into their office and asked one simple question: "How are you doing?" It was a moment of truth between the two of them where they connected, not just as *colleagues* but as *humans* feeling mutual compassion. What they had done wasn't easy. There would be other hard decisions needing to be made. But that day, the two of them created a bond of trust and understanding that would see them through.

Greater interdependence and compassion require that we evolve our approach to leadership. There's a vast difference in what counts as "results" when you move from being an independent contributor to being a leader. Take a look at the road map below and identify where you are right now in your journey to become a more compassionate leader:

THE ROAD MAP TO COMPASSIONATE LEADERSHIP

INDIVIDUAL CONTRIBUTOR	TEAM CONTRIBUTOR	TEAM LEADER
Acquiring skills, broadening experience & growing competence	*Growing experience & knowledge, problem-solving*	*Enabling work, monitoring, coaching, troubleshooting*
1-year horizon	2-year horizon	3-year horizon

DIRECTOR / DEPT. HEAD	VICE PRESIDENT	CEO / EXECUTIVE DIRECTOR
Track record precedes you, expert at resourcing & obstacle clearing, problem setting	*Seasoned, innovator, risk mitigator, people developer, connector*	*Wisdom, strategic, trust keeper, safeguarding, chief talent officer*
4-year horizon	5-year+ horizon	10-year+ horizon

In our early roles as *compassionate individual contributors*, we work hard to acquire skills, broaden our experience, and grow competence. In this phase, we often fly below the radar, expanding our depth of knowledge. If we've learned well, our efforts are noticed. Our next step is to become a *compassionate team contributor*, where we apply hard-fought experience, collaborate with team members, and gain perspective.

Next, we become *compassionate team leaders*. This crucial step sees our individual contributions subsumed to enable the work of others. Some leaders fail to make it past this pivotal moment; they just can't seem to let go of their role as "expert." The thing is that the "experts" are now working with you. Your role moves to becoming a compassionate listener who sets challenging but achievable goals and objectives. Your team values your ability to translate their concerns into reasonable action plans. You are respected as a trusted troubleshooter and someone who can overcome obstacles.

The next phase of your evolving leadership is to become a *compassionate director or department head*. You will achieve this because of the sterling track record you have amassed. You know how to hear others. You coach them to find their own solutions. A caution: you may feel at this juncture that you've become jaded. At this point in your evolution, it's vital to revisit your purpose story. Ask yourself, "Why did I become a leader anyway?" And to complicate things, the field becomes more crowded as high-performing leaders like you compete for the attention of upper management. While all of this is going on, you will experience failures in one form or another. While it may sound counterintuitive, this is a good thing. It is your emotional maturity and ingenious responses to setbacks that will distinguish you from others. These will take you to your next level of advancement.

Build bridges, master stamina, amass a sparkling track record, and develop resiliency at the director or department-head level, and it just may get you to the role of *compassionate vice president*. You'll know you are ready for this role when you are seen as representing not just your department but the welfare of the entire organization. You understand how all the organizational portfolios fit together. And you work hard to stop the turf wars that stifle innovation. You have created real—not synthetic—fellowship with your peers. I can't tell you how many organizations I've worked with that still have excellent individual

VPs as contributors but fail to have a healthy executive team who are all pulling in the same direction.

The final leg of your evolution—should you choose it—is to become a *compassionate CEO*, the ultimate caregiver of the organization. CEO roles are complex and multifaceted, but they have one thing in common: they are rooted in selflessness. Embodying the accumulated wisdom of experience and translating it to nurture healthy communication and relationships is a sacred responsibility. Relational CEOs take on the role of chief people officer, superb at recruiting, nurturing, and retaining the best talent. They are also exemplary coaches and mentors. To lead effectively at this level, you need to become a voracious reader and trend hunter at the leading edge of forces that may impact your sector.

INTERDEPENDENT ROLES OF LEADERS AND FOLLOWERS

As you accumulate mastery in these roles, you will develop a growing compassion for followers who will need equal measures of autonomy and support to carry out their work. To navigate this part of the leadership path, you need to support the overall health of the team. You will be judged by how effectively you coach, motivate, and support the team, especially when things aren't going according to plan.

To make the big shift from the individual focused on "ends" to a team leader dedicated to the "means" of getting there, leaders need to develop a sixth sense of who might be struggling and why. Leaders need to ferret out conflict and its source. Compassionate leaders are able to read the room. One way to do this is to turn back to our 3 Ps. Take a pause before you enter each meeting—whether you'll be physically opening the meeting room door or opening up a Zoom meeting. Breathe deeply, centre yourself, and rid your mind of noise and clutter. The busier you are, the more important it becomes to design premeeting routines that ensure you are focused on only one thing when you walk into that meeting room—the needs of your team.

As you plan for these encounters, facilitate moments of compassion by keeping emotions in check. Anxious, angry leaders breed cultures of fear (and loathing). Jealous leaders enflame infighting, while passive or bored leaders create a culture of low morale. And when we're fixated on our own emotions, we're unable to pick up on the feelings of others. By pausing and preparing for critical moments, you'll be in a much better place to prepare for and anticipate sentiments, feedback, and insights that arise from meetings.

COMPASSION DRIVES RESULTS

In addition to compassion being the right and human response, it also has a positive boomerang effect on your own leadership. EY, one of the top five consulting firms in the world, created the EY Belonging Barometer[22] to better understand the critical role that belonging plays in retaining employees, enhancing collaboration, and driving business performance. Its research suggests that for 41% of working adults, their workplace is where they feel the greatest social belonging. It's concerning that the researchers found that 75% of working adults felt excluded at work. The study also uncovered that over half of respondents felt they couldn't share, or were reluctant to share, dimensions of their identity at work. This research supports the need for leaders to become more intentional about creating a sense of belonging. The more we are able to help people feel safe and included, the faster we are able to attain goals and achieve stronger results.

A key ingredient to creating a sense of belonging is to become an active and compassionate listener. Leaders who pay attention to *how* people are saying things—the words they choose and how they share their concerns—are quicker to pick up on signs that the team may be, say, unclear about expectations or fearful about meeting an important deadline. You'll know you're on the right track when your focus on others has helped facilitate a clear expression of their thoughts—and in the process they have helped you crystallize your own.[23]

By proactively advocating for everyone's rights to be heard, we engage and empower others. This practice moves from cultivating project-focused teamwork to fostering a more holistic sense of belonging. As we acknowledge others' ideas, dilemmas, and concerns, we democratize culture and decrease politics and gossip. We avoid making people feel like outsiders in their own organization. Once we learn these skills, we are then able to coach those around us in becoming more empathetic listeners.

While being more understanding at work is a good thing to do, there's also a strong business case to be made for adopting this behaviour. Brené Brown, a well-known researcher and expert on compassion, found that when leaders practice compassion, they produce a more productive and happier workplace.[24] Compassionate leaders outpace other leaders because they are able to quickly aggregate diverse viewpoints. They train themselves to listen actively, digest information efficiently, extrapolate options, and then—and only then—draw conclusions. In fact, my research uncovered that the more a leader is able to absorb and reflect the values and sentiments of the team, the more the team will trust them to lead. And when we advocate for employees, they will do the same for us. And what this does is allow the team to rise above the pettiness and squabbling that happen when people feel they aren't being included in major decisions. Take this course, and you will make faster, more informed, and ultimately better decisions.

When I was interviewing leaders, I heard many stories of how they led compassionately. One that struck me particularly was Gaëtane Verna's discussion about ambition and compassion and how these change as a leader matures. As she looked back, she said, "When I first arrived in Toronto, I didn't know too many people. But now, The Power Plant is my country, and I need to defend that nation and find ways to inspire people to be just as compassionate as I am."

The way Gaëtane created this bond was to unite people in what she called her *social ambition*: "the responsibility I have to the people of Toronto, to my team, or government leaders. It's all about celebrating our collective values." Gaëtane believes it was her constant demonstration of good listening that galvanized her team to exceed expectations. She talked about the importance of being vulnerable and sharing moments of truth that were painful in her life: "I'm always going to share all my experiences because I want people to rise above and to succeed. I realized that every conversation you have with somebody can move people to move forward together." Gaëtane's compassion paid off. Thanks to her patient and steady listening, she empowered a strong and resilient team that was able to build a profile and reputation and develop new audiences to appreciate contemporary art.

FACILITATING VULNERABLE CONVERSATIONS DRIVES COMPASSIONATE LEADERSHIP

The ability to facilitate conversations is one of the most vital skills of compassionate leaders. This has come up time and again in my own work. Let me give you an example.

During my studies, toward the end of a Skype call with one of my thesis advisors, Liz Fulop, she commented that I hadn't given enough thought to the "other" in my work. *I thought* I had devoted plenty of time to the subject, but to Liz, I wasn't quite there.

Back then, I thought I was an advocate of others, but I can now see that the concept hadn't yet sunk in. That very same night, as Gordon and I were about to head to bed, I recapped my frustration, mimicking Liz's accent in the process.

Suddenly, hearing myself retell the story out loud to Gordon, something unlocked. After three years of my advisors pushing me to consider others more compassionately, I experienced my first true glimmer of what the compassionate practice was all about. I had an aha moment. I had alienated Liz—considered her "other"—by the way I talked about her accent. I had put a gap between the two of us. I knew I was onto something because of how uncomfortable I felt still staring at my alarm clock at 4:00 a.m. With that jolt, my understanding about othering grew. Acknowledging this shortcoming helped me to change my behaviour. It was a moment of truth I'll never forget. I'm now so grateful to Liz for seeing what I was lacking and pushing me on this point. She was practicing what she preached.

Researcher Robyn Stratton-Berkessel found that by asking positive—rather than neutral—questions, we can better make connections with people to form more positive relationships. Why might this be? Asking deeper questions opens up compassionate understanding and relatability. Her work uncovered that we can surface up to fourteen positive emotions in a person just by asking the right kind of question. By uncovering others' emotions, we're in a better position to help and support them. We gain insights into what motivates them, what they might be fearful of, or what's keeping them up at night. Her research cited the example of a father picking up his son after school and asking the age-old question "What happened in school today?"

The response is predictable: "Not much." But if the dad were to ask, "What's the best thing you learned in school today?" he'd get a much different response.[25]

So, let's delve into what those ideal questions are.

A CASE FOR ASKING BETTER QUESTIONS

The Princess Margaret Hospital Foundation (PMHF) is one of Canada's smallest but mightiest cancer charities. With a team of seventy-five, now-retired CEO Paul Alofs raised $1.2 billion. Comparable charities usually have more than two hundred people—and raise less money. How did Paul do it? The answer rests in his ability to see what matters to people and ask the right questions. He could see that corporate speak inspired no one, so he changed his approach. He began to ask a different kind of question: what I came to call "the compassion question." In the story below, we see how Paul made it a point to get to know everyone on his team intimately. The key here is that he was able to fuse their passion with the organization's mission. By doing this he inspired them to channel their energy into their work.

> Part of our secret sauce is that I know everybody in this place. I talk about our eight building blocks of culture: creed, culture, brand, resources, strategy, persistence, management, and leadership. We need to move beyond committee speak when developing vision, mission, and values. Nobody cares. They're dull, they're uninteresting, they're uninspired.
>
> One that impressed me was Johnson & Johnson's credo. It hasn't changed. It's always the same. And that company has been phenomenally successful. On one page they say here's what the business is all about. Here's our priorities. And here's how we go forward.
>
> That idea of the creed, as a way to focus the passion, prompted me to ask a five-second question: "What do you truly believe in, what is your promise

to the world?" When I speak about these things, most people are interested and they say, "You know, I need to do something."

We have many people who are leading with a science and mathematical background. Some are more successful than others, and I ask, "What do they do that's different?" Why is Geoff Hinton* attracting all of these people? He created a field of science, but more importantly, he's created a movement. All these guys who were running major social media outlets around the world, all work in his lab. The guy is a one-man, passion-capital success story. He's balanced technology and passion. When people bring their positive emotions to work, they put them to work.

—Paul Alofs, retired CEO,
Princess Margaret Hospital Foundation

THE FIVE-SECOND QUESTION

Paul's "five-second question" revealed what excited team members the most. Whether they had experienced cancer themselves, become a new parent, were learning a new language, or helping the homeless, Paul knew that. He then used that information to connect their passion to the company's cause. What I love about this example is how simple it is. This does not take years of practice. It takes thinking of the relevant question, taking the time to ask it, listening carefully to the answer, and then helping team members to channel that passion into their everyday work.

In Paul's case, the death of his mother to cancer was what prompted him to join PMHF. As Paul shared with me, he could have become

---

* Dr. Geoff Hinton is a fellow of computer science at the University of Toronto, where he is now an emeritus distinguished professor. His research in Toronto made major breakthroughs in deep learning that revolutionized AI, speech recognition, and object classification. In 2023, Hinton resigned his position as vice president and engineering fellow at Google out of concern about the harm that may be created by ChatGPT: hallmark behaviour of a relational leader.

negative, but it was finding what he called the *alchemy of adversity* that helped him to move forward. Channeling his passion to cure cancer pulled him out of a victim mindset and enabled him to become a motivating force for good. Paul shared this story not only with his team but also with audiences around the world. By sharing his vulnerability, he sets the tone for others to be open with him. As we see in this example, sharing a little information goes a long way in creating connections that make the cause real for others.

On a side note, Paul's story is also a good example of the importance of positive energy. When leaders radiate positive energy, it catches on. Paul said that anybody he knows who is a good leader has had really tough, bad things happen to them. But these leaders received compassion from colleagues, friends, and family that helped them fight another day. In turn, they were able to spread that compassion to others. From his own experience, Paul developed his mantra: "Out of bad comes good."

THE QUESTION THAT INSPIRES TEAM COMPASSION

Marnie Spears, CEO emerita of KCI, has developed an approach in her team meetings that allows her to "viscerally know what's happening." Carving out time at each meeting for people to openly share issues and concerns, she created what she calls Coaches Corner. Like Paul, she asks open-ended questions. She then listens deeply to understand how she can better clear a path and remove obstacles.

> We're always putting ourselves in the moment. We ask what questions we would want to ask a client and what kind of behaviour we should be striving for in certain situations. I talk to my executive team about where they're at right now. We spend the next twenty minutes just talking about where they are in their head. You know, their motivation, their challenges. I ask, "What do you need from me?" You've got to take the temperature of your team to know what is really going on.

It's not about sending an email saying, "How are you doing?" It's being really present. Often in these meetings, out of nowhere, someone will raise an issue and it will click for the team. As they appreciate each other's challenges, best practices are shared. Light bulbs go on with a "Oh . . . now I get it. Now I understand what this person is going through. I understand the problem."

— *Marnie Spears, CEO emerita of KCI*

Marnie always has her antennae up; she actively *looks for* problems and then finds ways to open up conversations about how people are really feeling. She's also on the lookout for common themes. She's always meticulously connecting the dots, helping people see they are not alone and that there are solutions to these common challenges. The twenty-minute conversation helps Marnie see who needs coaching and mentoring.

Marnie's team leaves their meetings feeling relieved ("Whew, I'm not the only one with this problem!"), confident ("I've found a way out of a sticky situation"), and committed ("I know I can call on my colleagues when I have a problem and they'll help me"). Marnie's approach helps her team not only reduce stress levels but also achieve their goals.

While it's great for leaders to be asking good, positive questions, it doesn't always mean that people will be open to sharing. People may be shy and introverted. Some have a firm line between "work" and "home" and what they are willing to talk about. Others may be untrusting, feeling that what they divulge may later embarrass or be used against them. Leaders need to meet people where they are. As we saw in Paul and Marnie's stories, they proactively sought out conversations—they didn't wait for people to come to them. They also shared with me that it was important to demonstrate that they could keep a confidence, that if someone shared something, "it was in the vault." Being patient with others is also vital to building compassion, and this isn't as easy as it sounds. While leaders are continuously in motion, it's important to walk around the office, having informal chats on how things are going. If you work in a virtual organization, make it a point to call people before or after meetings to check in on them. Ask the five-second question, have the twenty-minute chat with a team. Do this and you will energize and empower a team that is connected, trusts one another, and has a unified purpose.

We saw in the stories of Paul Alofs, Marnie Spears, and Gaëtane Verna that these were leaders who weren't satisfied with simply getting the job done; they wanted to start a movement! They accomplished this by celebrating each person's unique gifts and skills. I work with so many leaders today who don't even know whether or not members of the team have kids. They don't know their hobbies or whether they're supporting an aging parent. By knowing who you are working with, you'll be much better able to channel their passion with your organization's purpose.

Being a compassionate leader means balancing the unique tension between vulnerability and assuredness. It means shattering the mirror that reflects our individual needs and opening a window to facilitate true colleagueship. When you share your core beliefs, it creates the foundation for others to share theirs. Be the leader who asks for feedback, and take it to heart.

PRACTICE BECOMING MORE COMPASSIONATE

Here are the seven step-by-step practices you can use to grow compassion toward others:

- **Step 1: Assess your own compassion first.** Does compassion come easily and spontaneously to you? Are you naturally curious about others and their experiences? Or reluctant to engage in personal conversations with colleagues? What may cause you to resist acknowledging or being with those who are suffering? Are you shy? Do you not want to be intrusive? Or are you uncomfortable? Ask yourself under what conditions you might judge, dismiss, or minimize the hurt of others. Once you better understand what's holding you back, you can create a plan for being more intentional. Understand where you are most vulnerable yourself. Check in with people when you are feeling unsure of yourself, and don't be afraid to say you don't have all the answers.

- **Step 2: Take breaks.** Develop daily rituals to recharge and stay positive. Take a screen break and go for a ten-minute walk. Clear your mind. Think about what's gone well today. Focus on building up positive energy by jotting down three things you are grateful for. Reflect on those things and all the good in them. Break the tension that comes with the intensity of the job by taking time to wander around. You might be surprised to meet a colleague in the coffee shop who has a compassionate story to share.

- **Step 3: Ask positive questions.** Set up a weekly meeting or set aside part of a regular meeting to ask open-ended questions that encourage your colleagues to share their passion or bring their whole selves to work. Asking team members to respond to questions like "What is one of your proudest moments working here?" helps open up heartfelt conversations.

- **Step 4: Reach out and share.** Create a ritual by calling a colleague once a week, perhaps someone you haven't spoken to for a while. You'll be surprised by how your energy surges and moves you to a more compassionate state.

- **Step 5: Read the room.** Reading body language, mood, and tone can provide you vital information about the levels of commitment and quality of communication going on. Be on the lookout for four types of behaviour: those who present solutions and ideas for moving things forward, the naysayers or opponents, the followers, and the bystanders. You'll start to see patterns emerge. Once you've identified them, you can use your compassion practice to better understand their positions and build solutions that will encourage buy-in.

- **Step 6: Create psychological safety and well-being.**
  Develop self-awareness to help you better understand
  the emotions and feelings of others. Genuinely care and
  check in with others; ask whether they feel listened to,
  and encourage people to freely ask questions. Set clear
  expectations and goals; cocreate ground rules about when
  it's OK to introduce new ideas and/or challenge ways of
  doing things. Define together what's allowed—and what's
  not allowed. Allow people to challenge the status quo.
  Start meetings by sharing risks you may have taken, so
  others can share vulnerable moments too. Give people the
  freedom to disagree and facilitate conversations so that
  once the debate is over, everyone will commit to an idea
  or direction—even if it's not theirs.

- **Step 7: Cascade new behaviour.** Share your new practices during team meetings, encouraging everyone to
  create their own practices and providing time and a
  framework for doing so.

Evaluate Your Performance

As you develop your practice in compassion, ask yourself these questions:

- What am I most passionate about?

_____

_____

_____

- How am I making time to hear about others' passions?

_____

_____

_____

- How am I facilitating formal and informal communications to ensure everyone is heard and respected?

_____

_____

_____

- How can I inspire passion in others?

- Would people say they feel that our meetings are a safe space to share their thoughts?

- How am I facilitating psychological safety?

- What behaviours are helping me connect with the team?

- Are there behaviours I should change or stop that are hurting my relations with others?

  _____

  _____

  _____

- How are the needs of my team changing, and am I keeping up with them?

  _____

  _____

  _____

- During times when I haven't been as compassionate as I should be, have I made amends?

  _____

  _____

  _____

- What am I doing now to become more compassionate?

  _____

  _____

  _____

CHAPTER 4

Practice Empowered Learning

If you asked 99% of CEOs in January [2020] if they could transition their entire company to be 100% remote inside of a week, they'd say, "No, that's impossible." But suddenly the impossible became the possible.[26]

—*Stewart Butterfield, CEO, Slack*

Organizational learning will never be the same now that we've moved through the pandemic. As Stewart Butterfield points out, the reason things became "possible" was that leaders were forced to smash bottlenecks and cut bureaucratic red tape. It didn't matter where you stood in the pecking order—if you had a good idea on how to fix things, it was quickly elevated to decision-makers, embraced, and implemented. Organizations went on a learning frenzy: they shared intelligence quickly, experimented furiously to determine what worked and what didn't, and then continued to pivot as needed. Let's look at a situation where a leader was derailed because he failed to appreciate this big change.

After only eight months in the job, Mayo Schmidt, CEO of Nutrien, was unceremoniously sacked. During his brief tenure, Schmidt had apparently been hard to get a hold of and rarely in Canada, preferring his residence in Las Vegas. Reports of an "imperious" leadership style, being slow to get things done, and a toxic relationship involving his chief of staff later emerged as likely reasons for his departure. The impact was immediate. Nutrien—a $60 billion company—lost $2 billion in market value the day he was fired.

Schmidt had taken over from Chuck Magro, who had been known for empowering his staff with a coaching style that fostered a strong team spirit. He was well liked among his peers and had clearly built a strong culture. Joel Jackson, an analyst with BMO Capital Markets who covers Nutrien, reported that a "jarring change in corporate culture occurred" after Schmidt got the job.[27] Described by many as a "hard-ass" who rarely took counsel and internalized a ferocious focus on winning due to his time as a wide receiver for the Miami Dolphins, Schmidt didn't appear to care much about fitting in with Canadian business circles.

As recently as five years ago, this single-minded command-and-control behaviour might have been considered *distasteful* but *acceptable*, so long as it was accompanied by strong financial performance. But today, this kind of behaviour will get you fired. Schmidt either ignored or failed to read the importance of the empowered learning culture Magro had created. Maybe a good coach would have helped him.

HOW DO WE ACCELERATE LEARNING?

Today's learning is all about speed. Whether it's understanding how to become a better leader, learning new business models, or getting your mind around artificial intelligence, leaders must be well informed and willing to dig into complex new thinking. Though employees often have performance plans, what they really need are learning plans. This applies to everyone—from the CEO to the head of shipping. Being an empowered learner means that you know more than just your own subject area; it means you know what to do when you find yourself out of your depth and how to get up to speed. It means you know when to pause, how to plan, and to prepare.

This chapter will help you accelerate performance by showing you how to more effectively support employees who need to learn faster, overcome mistakes, and give those closest to the work the opportunity to take on new challenges. Equipping people with these kinds of skills will prepare your organization to handle major events like acquisitions, mergers, or big technology changes. According to a recent McKinsey study, 87% of organizations worldwide have noticed skill gaps; less than half of them know what to do about them.[28]

So many of the leaders I've talked to praise the coaches they work with—some tell me they wouldn't be the leader they are today without their coach. Ask these same leaders about their *own* coaching skills and that's a different story. Many confess they haven't taken the time to learn how to coach others. When leaders don't embrace strong coaching skills, not only are their people missing out on a lot of great learning opportunities, but these leaders are also threatening their organization's chances of thriving in a rapidly changing future.

Many leaders I've worked with start out as pseudo coaches, giving people "the solution" to their problems rather than helping their team member identify and thereafter come up with their own approaches. Don't be the coach who short-circuits conversations and fails to listen with intent. This isn't coaching; it's "expediting," which often only makes matters worse by creating an unhealthy dependence on the leader.

A vicious cycle emerges where the employee feels disempowered and continually defers to the leader to get "answers." The leader becomes exhausted from trying to do two jobs—neither one well. And when everyone is always running to you for answers, permission, and decisions, you can't be strategic, and you can't do *your own* job well.

To get out of the weeds and empower your team, take the compassion you learned in the previous chapter and apply it to your coaching stance. Your job is not to give people all the answers; it's to help them see—and become—the person they wish to be.

Certainly, there's good reason to get moving. A recent Gallup study showed that an empowered workforce can add 21% to profit and 20% to sales and can contribute to there being 70% fewer safety incidents.[29] And there's even better news. Empowering learning increases engagement and enhances the employee experience. We've seen a lot of examples of "mass empowerment" recently with the rise in "upskilling." Companies like AT&T, for example, have invested millions identifying where every job function is headed and providing people with the training required to prepare for those roles. In other companies, we see employees walking around with tablets as they interface with customers, empowered to make decisions and solve problems on the spot.[30]

To achieve these levels, leaders need to become better coaches. The same Gallup study revealed only four out of every ten employees agree they have been provided with opportunities to learn and grow. Making matters worse, employees gave a score of –25 (yes, that's right, minus twenty-five) when asked to rate their leaders' ability to provide opportunities for professional learning and development.[31]

COACHING LEADS TO BETTER LEARNING

These statistics make a powerful case for the development of coaching skills as a competitive advantage rather than as an item to check off on this year's performance appraisal. With budgets tightening at a time when organizations need avid learners, the relational practice of this chapter is an opportunity to make significant gains without spending a ton of money. Effective coaching empowers employees to learn on their own and arrive at their own solutions. It's an investment that has huge potential benefits over the long term.

These leaders don't tell, yell, or sell people on a prescribed way of doing things—or of learning.

They happily relinquish control and become more of a "guide on the side." People need and want to find their own solutions. The payoffs are clear: people who are coached to map their own journey find their destinations faster. Leaders who coach their teams well attract and retain the best employees. They nurture hotbeds of creativity and innovation.

Think about the jobs where you learned the most. I'll bet you a latte that these were the roles where you felt the most satisfied. And I'll also venture that you still keep in touch with that special person who made a commitment to you, to develop your skills, to be there when you needed support. It's these leaders, those who give more than they receive, that feel the most rewarded.

According to Sir John Whitmore, a leading figure in coaching, the definition of coaching is "unlocking a person's potential to maximize their own performance. It is helping them to learn rather than teaching them."[32] Organizations with strong coaching cultures boost not just individual but also organizational performance, grow accountability, improve employee engagement and retention, and create high performance, according to a 2019 study by the International Coaching Federation.[33]

While this may seem like common sense to most of us, it's surprising how many leaders' knee-jerk response is to "fix" the problems of others rather than asking good questions to help them draw their own conclusions. In one organization I worked with, the boss insisted that in each one-on-one meeting people bring in detailed status reports, which they would then go through with a red pen and painstakingly "correct"! Imagine how demoralizing that would be for the person sitting there. And imagine knowing that this would go on week after week. Not exactly a retention strategy, is it?

Wouldn't it have been better for the boss to request the report ahead of time, review the status, and then ask good questions about areas where they sensed the person could use some help? We've already seen the power of the five-second and twenty-minute questions, and in this chapter we'll be exploring six kinds of questions you can ask to coach individuals and teams to success.

It may seem like an oxymoron, but as you ask these questions, you're working to create a climate of *interdependent autonomy*. This is a hallmark of relational leadership, where people feel free to do their work while respecting that everyone's work is interconnected. Great coaches connect the dots for people. Many teams have told me about making a decision they felt was "completely logical" only to find that it created shock waves in other departments. By helping people appreciate the interplay between independence and interdependence, coaches empower cross-functional team learning.

This kind of coaching also supports people to successfully "fail forward." Show me a culture where people are blamed and shamed when things go wrong, and I'll show you an organization starved of creativity and innovation. Teams need to feel they won't be hung out to dry if they try something different and it doesn't go perfectly the first time. It's up to leaders to let everyone know that so long as projects are heading in the right direction, *and* teams are learning along the way, no one will be punished or, worse yet, fired. Failing forward means using our mistakes to help us grow and not being afraid to take future risks. By having coaching conversations that focus on learning from what went wrong, leaders are helping people to make better future decisions.

Empowering the team involves communicating the benefits of learning and having the means to reward it. You will know your coaching is successful when people start requesting support to go back to school, attend a conference, or do volunteer work. So make sure that your coaching efforts are supported by recompensing efforts and incentivizing performance. In this way, you'll start to see not only a healthier workplace but also a more innovative one. The benefits of coaching can be life-changing for the people you support by reducing stress, boosting creativity, improving communication, and building confidence. Significantly, coaching clarifies and aligns goals and objectives to achieve results as well as accelerating productivity and facilitating teamwork.

THE HOW-TO OF RELATIONAL COACHING

You may be wondering what the difference is between traditional coaching and relational coaching. The key difference lies in incorporating four types of reflection into your coaching practice. When I was about halfway through my studies, I had an aha moment when I was able to connect the four ways we reflect to the practice of relational coaching. The good news is that these skills won't be foreign to you. We use them every day. We use *inquiry* to better understand the world, we use *rehearsal* to practice for important meetings, we use *introspection* to better understand ourselves and others, and we use *spontaneity* to quickly get into action when the moment calls for it.

That said, we need to practice before we unleash these concepts on unsuspecting individuals and teams. That's why it's a good idea to strike up a peer coaching group in your organization. Not only will you develop your abilities, but you'll also be helping each other by participating in real-time coaching.

The first skill, *inquiry*, is the place where we continually source, collect, assemble, sort, and make sense of all the information around us. Coach people to curate, collect, and catalyze information, as these are some of the most important skills employees need to become better learners. Helping your coachee understand when they have enough information to make a decision or take that next step is the vital work here. Your support will help them find the balance between getting enough information to make an evidence-formed decision and drowning in data that leads to analysis paralysis, where decisions are never made. When we use inquiry, we help others harness data to drive insights.

Rehearsal, the ability to prepare ahead of time for critical moments of truth, is the most underestimated of all the reflective skills. By coaching people to pause, plan, and prepare, you will guide them to use their experience to "try on" various solutions and apply them. Helping people learn the art of rehearsal lays the groundwork for everything from making presentations to having critical conversations that hit the mark. As leaders, we want to build in enough time and safe space to provide feedback to continually improve a team's approach before they "go live." Too many of us only use rehearsal when we are preparing for important speeches or crucial meetings. In our fast-paced world, rehearsal gives us time to step back and consider scenarios that might emerge, then anticipate and better prepare for the challenges that may lie ahead.

Introspection encourages people to go deep inside themselves to reflect on past experiences. It's also the place where they can share dreams about the future, take stock of their life, determine what they need to learn, and map out ways to get there. As you're coaching people to become more introspective, it's helpful to refer back to practices we learned to become more self-aware. A mantra that relational coaches embrace is that "We are all leading all the time." No matter where your coachee sits in the organizational chart, urge them to develop their leadership purpose story; ask them questions about their passion. If you're coaching someone through a difficult incident, ask them questions about what triggered their response and what they would do differently next time. Empowered learners should feel safe to admit when they've made mistakes, and your help in analyzing what went wrong will strengthen them. When we use introspection, we help others reveal to themselves what they need to learn.

Finally, there's *spontaneity*. Think back to a moment when you were flying by the seat of your pants and pulled off a win. You'll recall that feeling of achieving something pretty special. It was just you and your team—and your combined experience and knowledge of each other's strengths and weaknesses—that brought on success. This is where using spontaneity as a tool to coach makes all the difference. When we encourage others to experiment, to be in flow with the moment, we help them to develop greater agility and think on their feet.

As I work to develop leaders' coaching skills, I've noticed that the ones who stand out are adept at toggling between two elements of spontaneity. They know how to reflect *in the moment*, "watching themselves" perform various tasks while they're happening. And they know how to reflect *on the moment*—that is, after the event is finished, they have a process in place to analyze and distill what happened, how they behaved, and what needs to change. As you coach team members to develop this skill, encourage them to take micropauses during intense work so that they are better able to reflect and pivot while performing. You want them to literally get a "feel" for what a situation requires so that they can become accustomed to the pace and pressure of spontaneity.

By coaching people to embrace the four reflective skills, you'll help them drive insights and become better prepared, more aware of when they need help (and not afraid to ask for it), and more at ease when they undertake brand-new assignments. As a relational leader you want to keep the cycle going—when you build in inquiry, rehearsal, introspection, and spontaneity to your coaching practice, you're empowering your teams to make faster, more informed decisions that deliver projects on time and on budget.

THE QUALITIES OF AN EMPOWERED COACH

There is a myriad of excellent books out there on coaching, and as I reviewed in them the behaviours and best practices of what it takes to be a solid coach these days, these were the major skills that repeatedly surfaced.

The first was developing an *honest and safe rapport* with the person or team being coached.

Listening and empathy follow hard on the heels of creating this zone of safety; it's been said that a good coach doesn't talk much but is an active and engaged listener.

The most successful coaches *pose specific questions* depending on the circumstances. They want to get to the heart of the matter, as quickly and as efficiently as possible. Having said this, a good coach never makes the person they are coaching feel rushed. Allow space to think out loud, and only when all ideas are on the table should you begin to offer insight.

Coaches are natural-born givers, and this leads to the next practice: *they contribute far more than they take away* from conversations. Relational coaches are constantly on the lookout for moments to help coachees see things in a different light or explore a problem in a way they haven't thought of before. This means harvesting your experiences in new ways. The last thing you want to be doing is regaling your coachee with your own hero stories. Instead, figure out how your experiences can inspire just the right question to help the person gain a different perspective.

A great coaching encounter is marked by the coachee experiencing what we will call a "teachable moment" that causes them to change.

The litmus test of a good coach is that they can *spot teachable moments*. These inflection points are often characterized in two ways: the first is that moment when the light bulb goes on and the person feels newly empowered. They might arrive at a particular solution, understand something from a new perspective, feel clear on the path ahead. These are the times when we help people to become their best selves.

The second (and more common) teachable moment happens when shit hits the fan. When you hear that you're being invited to a "critical incident review" or a "strategic assessment review," that's code for "we can never do that again." Coaching in these moments requires a compassionate touch. When you're trying to get to the "truth" or "nut" of something, there are usually a lot of people ducking for cover and a lot of bruised egos in the room. It's at these times that your coaching facilitation skills will be tested. Recall our action steps from the previous chapter on creating psychological safety. It's often better to approach these situations one-on-one to get an understanding of various perspectives before you bring the team together. You want to make sure to create the conditions where people can accept what's happened but also move beyond it. Otherwise, people act defensively, point fingers, or—worse yet—are in denial.

Finally, coaching means helping people to *commit to new courses of action*. Summarize what has been discussed at the end of each meeting and, importantly, write it down. That way when you have your next conversation, you'll be able to easily pick up the threads.

PERFORMANCE COACHING VERSUS DEVELOPMENT COACHING

There are two types of coaching: performance coaching and development coaching. I like to call performance coaching the science of coaching: it is there that leaders support individuals who are having trouble reaching a strategic goal, perhaps because of a lack of experience and/or knowledge in a specific hard skill. Development coaching, on the other hand, is an art, where leaders explore leadership concepts like interpersonal relations, power, politics, communications, team development, and peer relations. Most leaders need to engage in both these forms of coaching to varying degrees.

Let's look at coaching observations from Wes Hall, chairman and founder of WeShall Investments Inc., Kingsdale Advisors, and the BlackNorth Initiative. Wes explained that he was developing his own coaching style to help people pivot, invent, improvise, and execute *si-multaneously*. In Wes's view, *soft skills* like communication, empathy, and vulnerability had become the new *hard skills*: As he put it, "Now, no matter where you sit in the organization, you must demonstrate both." This means two things: putting an end to silos in "hard" and "soft" learning, and infusing strategic thinking into your coaching.

A good coach observes and listens intently to identify both the hard and soft areas to provide support. They may be focused on a work challenge but are also observing the person's body language to gauge how they're feeling about a particular topic. The coach is harnessing all their senses and skills to receive both the hard and soft information and using that to guide the conversation forward and determine the right questions to ask. A good coach is an expert question asker. Here's an exercise you can try next time you're coaching someone. Discipline yourself to only ask questions—don't give advice, don't consult. Just ask a question, wait for a response, and then ask another question. Try this out by posing these six different kinds of questions:

Miracle questions: Ask, "Suppose that while you're sleeping to-night a miracle happens, solving this long-standing problem. When you wake up in the morning, what would be different? Now that the problem is solved, what would you have changed in order to satisfacto-rily address the issue?"

Scaling questions: This form of questioning is helpful when you need to do a "temperature check" or "level set," which helps the coachee identify problems and helps you understand their severity. Invite the person to think about their problem on a continuum by ask-ing, "On a scale of 1 to 10, with 1 being the worst and 10 being the best, how would you rate our progress on this project?" Once you have the number, explore how the rating translates into action. If the person rates their progress as a 3, you might then ask, "What specifically is happening that prompted you to rank our progress at a 3?" Next, ask what would need to happen to rate the project between 6 and 7. Scaling questions can also be helpful for tracking a team's progress toward goals and monitoring incremental change.[34]

Presupposing change questions—focus on the positive: When people and teams are experiencing trouble on a project, they tend to focus on the negative. Often, though, there are a lot of positive things that might be overlooked, minimized, or discounted. Unearthing positive changes—no matter how small—is helpful in these circumstances. Ask, "What's different or better since the team last met?" Affirm the positive steps that have occurred, draw out the actions team members have taken to enhance or improve the situation. Using this good news as building blocks to keep the momentum going reminds people, "Look how far we've come."

Barometer questions: All you have to do is think of the classic Steve Jobs question, "Is this the best you can do?" When you want to turn up the pressure, the barometer question can be useful. As a leader, though, consider how it may affect your team. Some thrive in this kind of environment; others can become demoralized. You may wish to use a gentler form of this question, like "How can we do better to fix this problem?"

Exception questions: These questions provide an opportunity to identify times when conditions have been different for the person you are coaching. They help people see a positive outcome or recollect moments similar in nature to their current situation, allowing them to reflect on the feelings and behaviours that could help them overcome their problem. Examples of these kinds of questions are:

- Tell me about a time when you felt the happiest working on this project.
- What was it about that day that made you feel good?

Opposite questions: Rather than asking "Why should the team accept this?" ask "Why *shouldn't* they accept this?" The difference is, as you can see, the earlier question doesn't address team perspectives or individual priorities. By shifting the question, you also get the team to focus less on defending their ideas and more on advocating for them, addressing the obstacles that folks may take issue with, and trying to proactively solve those problems. In doing so, they become more solution focused.

STORYTELLING AS A WAY TO EMPOWER LEARNING

In my interviews with leaders, I came across four stories that illuminate how to empower team learning. As organizations seek new ways to help people learn faster, their leaders will need to become hyperlearners themselves and model curiosity, fearlessness, and an openness to making mistakes.

Rob MacIsaac shared a strategy he deployed when he first joined Hamilton Health Sciences as CEO. We can imagine how daunting it would be to reach out to 11,000 employees across multiple sites, so Rob hatched an innovative way to teach himself and have people teach each other. Deploying his mantra—"Leadership is about humble inquiry"—he created a video series where he asked questions and encouraged employees to *coach him.*

The YouTube series called *Teach Rob Your Job* went viral, building community and smashing down silos with each new view. Here was a chance for the entire hospital campus to not only better understand each other's jobs but also appreciate their interdependencies. One employee said, "I've worked here for thirteen years, and before I saw that [video], I had no idea what they did beyond those doors [referring to a lab that was just across the hall from where they worked!]."[35]

But Rob's learning didn't stop there. Seeing the success of his efforts, he built upon them. *Teach Rob Your Job* morphed into *Three Things You Should Know.* In this next series, he asked frontline workers, "What are the three most important things I should know about your job?" These "touchstone moments" not only inspired cross-organizational understanding but were also instrumental in developing the hospital's new strategy.

Rob shared with me that his executive team initially had some trepidation about his approach. They were concerned what might be revealed during these very public moments with a new leader. But as the videos were posted, anxiety dissipated, and they became better coaches in the process.

The second story is from Wendy Zatylny, who learned to empower teams to solve problems faster by using a technique called "presetting."

This breakthrough occurred while she was attending an executive development program at Ivey Business School. The facilitator asked the group to put together a three-dimensional puzzle with wooden pieces. The instructor told them they had two minutes. After a few tries the team got it down to thirty seconds. The facilitator kept pushing, urging the teams to shorten the time. Ultimately, they got it down to eight seconds.

It turns out the only thing that stops us is our *preset mindset*. Wendy described how the team "stopped themselves" at two minutes and then again when they got to thirty seconds. They thought they couldn't possibly go any further. As the facilitator kept moving the goalposts, the team continued to push themselves and go beyond what they'd initially thought they could do.

She described the group coaching process that evolved as the team worked to shave off seconds like this: "Normally, we were reaching for the puzzle piece, getting into position, and putting it into place. What we realized is we didn't have to wait. So, in presetting, I already had my hand on the puzzle piece. It was turned in the right direction. We established an order among the team as to who would go first, second, and on from that."

This was a moment of truth that transformed the group of individuals into a team. Initially, everyone wanted to place their puzzle piece first. With practice, they realized the order didn't matter, and they all made an equal contribution to the success of the team.

As Wendy described her experience, I imagined each team member settling in to play the game, perhaps thinking they possessed "the" unique insight or formula that would ultimately "solve" the puzzle. But what ended up happening was that the powers of rehearsal (doing the activity a number of times) and spontaneity (trying different things each time they did it) improved their time. Empowered learning became the link between time and experience.

Think about a similar exercise you could do with your team to help them learn the power of "presetting." Accelerate creative problem-solving by taking the team off-site. Visit your local college or university's digital media zone. Try bringing in guests and experts who see your challenges from very different viewpoints. I once heard of a retailer who brought in ballerinas and construction workers to help the company innovate their design of shoes. The simple act of reframing a problem can open up new ways to approach it.

As Wendy experienced, use the power of iteration—having the team approach a problem again and again. Ask them to pause and gain some distance from their approach, and then have them come back to have another go at it until they have exhausted all ideas. You can also encourage your team to break free of self-imposed "rules" that may be holding them back. Wendy's story shows us how changing up team activities can move us away from fixed mindsets to see new paths forward.

Michael Hirsh, CEO of WOW!, shared how coaching, mentoring, and job shadowing revealed new ways to grow his business.

Michael described a moment that changed the way he approached business development when he launched Nelvana's first fully animated show, *Cosmic Christmas*. He met an executive at Viacom, Jamie Kellner, who said, "Why don't you come and sit in my office for a few weeks and listen to me on the phone to hear how I sell your show?"

It was the most valuable thing he could have done. As he sat and listened to an expert in action, he learned how to sell better. "'Cause there's a rhythm to selling. And Jamie always had good advice. So, I had a great coach in him, and he went on to have a great career. We were one of the first production companies that got close to him; we learned the art of syndication from the master."

George Lucas was another mentor. Pixar was on the rise at that time, and Michael gained early insights into where the industry was going. "I was fortunate to have a few mentors. With Lucas it was less formal; we just hung out. He just knew that I would pick it up, that I'd hear what he was sharing with us; he saw something in me in the raw. 'Cause I was inventing how I was doing it. He [George] had been trained in a system."

Michael "picked up" a huge amount of valuable information from those informal conversations. These early experiences also shaped Michael's own coaching and mentoring style. Consider how informal occasions and job shadowing might be incorporated into your own coaching practice.

In our final story, Stephen Letwin, CEO of Mancal, uses the metaphor of "jump ball" to demonstrate spontaneous innovation in action. Stephen began by talking about how important it is for leaders to instill confidence in their team. He described that, early in his career, the coaches and mentors who believed in him had been the ones to help make him a more confident leader. And the more confident he became, the more empowered he felt to pay it forward. Confident leaders don't want or need to get hung up on the political side of things, and that ensures they remain more open and interested in new ideas.

One of the ways Stephen empowered team learning was to support what he called a healthy "jump ball culture." He explained, "The way it works is that even though a person can own a project, they may get absorbed into another one quite seamlessly. We let somebody who's got free time come in and work on any project. The team embraces this learning style without politics because they know their job is secure and their bonuses are there." Jump ball culture also encourages people to mentor and coach each other: as people come and go on a project, they are constantly bringing people up to speed, integrating their input, and hearing the fresh ideas that come from people who are new to the project. This new thinking can break logjams, bring fresh creativity, and shake things up when people may be fatigued.

We know sometimes a jump ball is won by the taller person, other times by the person who can jump the highest, but it is always won by the person who is *most prepared* for what is about to happen.[36] Critical to winning is finding focus inside the jump ball circle, always knowing where your teammates are. The key to keeping the learning going was ensuring a fluid and dynamic process that kept ideas rolling and encouraged substitution players, each with their own areas of expertise. When you next review the projects in your portfolio, consider how you might introduce "jump ball" to infuse new ideas and energy into the process.

PRACTICE EMPOWERED LEARNING

Here are seven practices you can use to grow your coaching capabilities to empower individual and team learning.

- **Step 1: Learn how to coach, and develop your coaching style.** Expose yourself to a variety of different coaching styles and methods to develop your own unique practice.

Develop a style that helps people see a positive future for themselves and grows their confidence in taking on ambitious challenges.

- **Step 2: Build your reflective skills.** Create a coaching discipline that harnesses the four different types of reflection: inquiry, rehearsal, introspection, and spontaneity.

- **Step 3: Give up power to empower.** Be the leader who shares information, encourages others to lead with confidence, and lets go of the need to control everything. Provide frequent updates on what's happening across the organization. Encourage people to join together in cross-functional teams to enrich the flow of information and build mutual understanding. Supply teams with resources to expand their knowledge, and provide continuous feedback.

- **Step 4: Empower teams to learn.** Begin by assessing individuals and then the strength of the team as a whole to identify learning needs; follow through with learning strategies. Encourage teams to move around to other projects to bolster cross-functional learning; reward and recognize growth mindsets that are driven by curiosity.

- **Step 5: Create teachable moments.** Be on the lookout for teachable moments such as broken links in accountability, missed deadlines, poor communication, fractured alignment, and defensiveness. Debrief projects and incidents to help people reflect *in* and *on* the moment; solicit examples for both individual and team learning; identify stretch assignments, mentors, and experts who can grow team learning.

- **Step 6: Create room for mistakes.** Once you've identified teachable moments, create a safe space for people to "fail forward" and to get back up and start again. Develop a work plan identifying specific activities that will help people stretch, learn, grow, and realize their potential. Host roundtables or kitchen-table conversations to push and pull at ideas. Identify who on your team is an expert—or invite guests in—and ask them to share their fuckups: where they did well and what they would do differently.

- **Step 7: Be patient and measure progress.** It takes time to see the benefits of coaching. Give yourself reasonable time horizons ranging between three months and a year. Check in with your coachee on a regular basis to track progress. Work with your coachee to identify goals and then make key commitments that will help them achieve those goals. The key here is that the coach and the coachee must be accountable to each other. Ask one another whether you're measuring the right things and what might be missing. Have open conversations about what's working well and not so well. Find out where strengths lie and develop professional development plans that span short-, medium-, and long-term horizons. There's a template to develop your coaching skills and track your progress that you can download on our website: DrJillBirch.com.

Evaluate Your Performance

As you assess your strengths in encouraging empowered learning, ask
yourself these questions:

- Who and what resources do I need to build up my coaching muscle?

  _____

  _____

  _____

- How am I consciously identifying teachable moments to support individuals?

  _____

  _____

  _____

- What are three learning goals our team needs to achieve? What is my plan to help them get there?

  _____

  _____

  _____

- Which one of the skills—inquiry, rehearsal, introspection, or spontaneity—am I most comfortable with? Which do I need to learn more about and practice?

- Where are the learning gaps—in individuals and the team—and how do I coach to help people find ways to close them?

- Is there a peer coaching group I can join to help me practice my skills?

- What measures have we identified to help us know we've achieved our learning goals?

CHAPTER 5

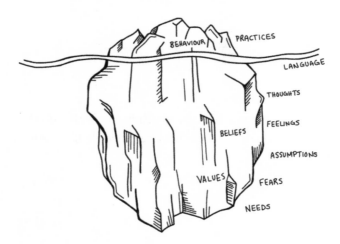

Practice Nurturing Culture

Culture is simply a shared way of doing something with passion.

—Brian Chesky, founder, Airbnb

People are attracted to workplaces that give them a sense of belonging; the more caring your culture is, the harder people will work and the more committed they will be. A caring culture knows what it stands for and puts its values of treasuring employees, customers, and stakeholders above all else.

Both big things and small things contribute to creating a caring culture. The tone at the top of the house sends signals to everyone about the culture espoused and the culture that really exists. I recently worked with an organization where the senior team claimed they had an open-door policy and believed in transparency. When I conducted focus groups with the staff, I was surprised to learn that the very team who said their door was "open" was actually housed on the top floor, accessible by swipe cards that only they possessed. That's a big promise gone terribly wrong. People quickly see through these claims, and this is why so many cultures today find themselves struggling.

There are demonstrable things that contribute to a caring culture—like good salaries and strong benefits packages—and there are expressions of caring such as handwritten notes of thanks or recognition. Leadership that supports employee well-being is an example of the compassion we talked about in chapter 3 and contributes to a healthy organization that empowers others.

It's up to leaders to ensure that the organizational culture is welcoming, supportive, and inclusive. If you're not doing the work that's required, trust me, your competition is—and if their culture is regarded as more attractive, you will not only lose your best employees, but you'll also have trouble attracting top talent to replace them.

I get queasy when I hear stories of leaders *building* culture like a LEGO set. People aren't simply inanimate pieces that you snap into place within an organization. They are always growing, evolving, and wanting to contribute in new ways. They want to weigh in on their workplace, and they often have great ideas about what could be done better. Many organizations pay lip service to the idea of culture—conducting endless employee engagement surveys—but then fail to do anything with the feedback. There's nothing worse than asking for feedback, raising expectations, and failing to deliver. When leaders unilaterally try to fashion culture in their own image, you end up with toxic cultures. For these leaders, culture is a power tool, used to justify imperatives that can lead to conformity in the form of negative, sabotaging behaviour.

You don't have to go far to see companies that "get" culture and those that don't. Take the story of Vishal Garg, CEO of Better.com, who announced in a three-minute Zoom that the nine hundred people on the call would lose their jobs immediately—right before the holiday season. Imagine the impact of this move on Better.com's culture. Would you want to work there?

At a time when employee belonging has been vital to nurturing culture, he fired the diversity, equity, and inclusion recruiting team.[37] Remaining employees allege that, in a subsequent meeting, he told them that their productivity would be closely tracked. As one staff member shared with *Fortune* magazine, "His tone was extremely harsh and threatening."[38]

After being universally condemned for his insensitivity, Garg was temporarily relieved of his duties and dragged off to take part in executive coaching. An independent review of Better.com's culture recommended respectful workplace training, expanded leadership, and a new ethics and compliance committee reporting directly to the board.

The damage caused by behaviours like this shows us how important it is to develop practices that build trust: the foundation of all caring cultures and an area we will be exploring in depth in this relational practice. Months after Garg's return, board members and five members of the executive team fled the company, citing "a lot of tension" as many employees who reported to them were laid off.[39]

Now ask yourself, even after learning of the new measures that were implemented at Better.com, would you want to work there? My guess is no. Their story is a tainted one. The lesson here is that once cultural values have been compromised, the road to building back trust is long and difficult.

There is a better way.

Now for a very different kind of story. During the pandemic, Unilever embarked on a daring transformation to address climate change and social inequality for the global markets it served. Founded in the 1880s, the company has consistently grown over the past thirty years. CEO Alan Jope instinctively knew that only by improving Unilever's *own* culture could they make good on these global commitments.

The organization began by declaring it would raise living standards in two areas: to ensure that everyone who directly provides goods and services to Unilever will earn at least a living wage or income by 2030 and that the company would help five million small- and medium-size enterprises grow their business by 2025.[40] Unilever also focused on another cultural hot button: the future of work. We've all seen stories out there about how divided workplaces are over return-to-work policies. The company stated that it would pioneer new models with flexible options by 2030. Putting a deadline that's seven years out means the company will approach the strategy by consulting, experimenting, evaluating, adjusting, and then consulting some more until they get it right. This is very much a relational process in action, one that is cocreated and ever emergent.

To bring this caring culture to life, the organization committed itself to leveraging the power of all employee capabilities; unlocking speed and agility; becoming a beacon for equity, diversity, and inclusion; and finally being "human, purposeful and accountable."[41]

So here's the million-dollar question: If you're a leader at Unilever, what might you do to actually bring these declarations to life? How do you show employees that you care and walk the talk? Eureka! Their idea was to engage all 150,000 of their employees to participate in workshops to discover and share their purpose story. A purpose story examines deep questions like "Who am I?" and "Why do I exist?" and "What do I care deeply about?"

You can imagine the virtual watercooler talk that spread throughout the company as groups of employees around the world all participated in this exercise. Employees made videos and shared their purpose story; as these individual stories accumulated, they became a uniting force that inspired collective energy. The key next step was for leaders to identify common themes that could then be woven into the cultural fabric.

Employees' stories became the foundation of the very qualities that Unilever sought to engender: flexibility, agility, and resilience. CEO Jope said these attributes would be needed to master Unilever's "inner game." It was only once this passion was harnessed internally that the company could strengthen what he called their "outer game." Did it work? The proof is in the numbers. Unilever's sales growth was 4.5%, its fastest in nine years.[42] Employee engagement scores improved from 74% in 2018 to 82% in 2021.[43]

The Unilever purpose story demonstrates that strong caring cultures spark the passion that drives not just financial performance but, most importantly, employee trust. Next time you embark on a strategic planning process, remember the Unilever story. By connecting the purpose of the company with the spirit of its people, a trust bond is formed that makes great things possible.

The symbiosis of purpose and trust underpin a strong culture.

When these two qualities are present in an organization, they mutually reinforce each other. A Gallup research study showed that a 10% improvement in employees' connection with mission or purpose leads to an 8.1% decrease in turnover and a 4.4% increase in profitability.[44] As a relational leader, it's your job to build that strong cultural foundation. You need to be asking your employees two vital questions: "Are you happy here?" It's a pretty simple question, and sometimes body language alone can speak volumes about how comfortable people are. And "What can I do to help you in your job?" As we saw in Rob MacIsaac's story, asking what could be done to make things better is a way to strengthen communication, dedication, and teamwork.

TRUST IS A CRITICAL BUSINESS ISSUE

Like leadership, trust has become a significant business issue. Even before the pandemic, a compelling case was made that trust was the most expensive commodity in the world. It takes a lot of time to nurture trust, but once squandered, it can take years to rebuild. The secret sauce is a leader's ability to cultivate and grow trust in small ways, like having a coffee with an employee to thank them for a job well done, and in big ways, like launching an organization-wide listening tour.

According to a *Harvard Business Review* study, the constructs of trust are fairly simple.[45] When people are authentically engaged and believe they are dealing with real people who care, they will trust you. When people have faith in the judgment of their leaders, they will trust you. And when people feel that you care about them, they will trust you. These are the unassailable precepts that build a caring culture. If you detect something amiss in your culture, *trust me*: it's because one of these principles has been violated.

We simply can't afford not to nurture caring cultures. And it's not just a "nice" thing to do. Compared with people at low-trust companies, those who work at high-trust companies report 74% less stress; 106% more energy; 50% higher productivity, 13% fewer sick days, 76% more engagement, 29% more satisfaction with their lives, and 40% less burnout.[46] If that doesn't make the case to invest in trust, I don't know what will.

In addition, consumer attitudes have shifted, with 90% of people believing brands must protect the well-being and financial security of their employees and suppliers.[47] And consumers have a big say, since they decide where to spend their money.

NAVIGATING INEVITABLE TENSIONS AND BUILDING TRUST

Determining how you will balance several tensions that exist in all organizational cultures is critical to the survival of your team. Nurturing trust is essential to managing these situations successfully.

First, you must acknowledge the tension you'll likely feel as you navigate the tricky business of giving people autonomy *and* providing support when they need it; this means giving people trust (once they are trained) and then letting them loose to make decisions within their sphere of control. There can be some hair-raising moments as you teeter between overseeing everything and giving people full authority. You may feel uncomfortable or anxious. Mastering how to monitor progress while providing autonomy takes time and practice. It helps to recognize that this might happen. It can help to let people know when you will be checking in and be clear about your expectations regarding timelines and milestones. Take the time to learn the rhythms of the team; this will go a long way toward building this form of trust.

Next, you must navigate the tension between encouraging people to share diverse opinions *and* fostering unity. This is where facilitation and communication skills come in. As you sharpen your observational skills, you will get better at recognizing when everyone has had enough time to get their oar in the water and when they are ready to row together as a team. Making people feel safe is key to facilitating openness and helping people listen to feedback.

Be that leader who builds a culture that is imbued with fair play *and* humility. Jeff Martin of Tribal Planet discussed the need for leaders to check what he called displays of "caustic honesty." These are cultures that pride themselves on eviscerating others, justifying their harsh words by saying, "Hey, don't take it personally." I once worked at a place where a VP prided themselves on telling their direct reports exactly how they felt about their performance. The VP often berated people in public settings, making an example of them to the rest of the group. This created such toxicity that my colleagues and I had no other recourse but to approach the president and say, "Enough is enough." This is the first step in confronting those with no filter. They need to be called out. The next thing is to insist they work with a coach for a minimum of six months. In our case, even the coaching didn't work, and ultimately the VP was let go.

Finally, you must find the balance between sparking agility and innovation and providing structure and consistency. Imagine the promise of a team of twenty happily colouring outside the lines but missing a key deadline. It happens. Having conversations ahead of time about milestones and key deliverables helps teams maintain that balance. Leaders who are able to toggle between those different modalities become valued trust keepers of the organization.

If culture is the collective coming together of people to a common cause, trust is the glue that holds them together. According to researchers Frances Frei and Anne Morriss, trust has three drivers: authenticity, logic, and empathy.[48] They encourage leaders to evaluate which of these drivers is most "wobbly" for them. To improve behaviour in each of these three areas, leaders should ask themselves these questions: "Are people experiencing the 'real' me?" and "Do I instill in people my belief that I know they can do whatever task they've been asked to do?" Lastly, ask yourself, "Do people believe I really care about them and their success?"

We only have to look at examples where these elements are out of sync to see that without trust there can be no caring culture. Think about the early days when Elon Musk became chief twit at Twitter. One employee described the company as a "free-for-all," where some people worked to ingratiate themselves to collaborate on projects dubbed "Elon critical" while others ran for the doors.[49] Losing trust means employees will turn on the very company that once so excited them. Precious energy gets swallowed up in lawsuits and public relations maneuvers.

The high cost of a lack of trust has been well documented in the Edelman Trust Barometer that each year tallies who is trusted, who has lost it, and ways to get it back. A chief finding in their 2021 study was that 54% of those surveyed said that CEOs must be held accountable to speak out on controversial issues they care about. A further 78% said they want CEOs to be much more visible when discussing public policy or work the company has done to benefit society.[50] If you're lying back thinking, "Whew, well I'm glad that's the CEO's problem," think again. If these demands are being made at the top, they will surely trickle down to you no matter where you sit in the organization. Be ready for them. As a relational leader, you'll want to start thinking now about actions you can take to support the culture to keep trust high.

What is culture to you? Defining culture has always been a challenge—informally, some people will say it's "how things are done around here." If that's the kind of definition you're using in your organization, you may be giving people permission to behave badly. Unethical or caustic behaviour may be excused because *that's the way we roll here.*

A way I like to define culture is this: anchored by a compelling vision, culture is a coming together of shared values that builds alignment toward a common purpose.

As I speak with teams, they are becoming increasingly concerned about the process of nurturing culture—often reduced to the "yearly retreat" with the requisite issuance of plasticized wallet cards listing key values along with posters in the lunchroom. A second issue employees raise is that they see culture-building as commoditized branding exercises for outside consumption. While the values we codify like excellence, integrity, agility, equity, and transparency are legit, what actually happens to them after the sticky notes are peeled off the walls? Creating a culture based on stories and storytelling helps keep these values alive. One CEO I spoke with said that he now facilitates quarterly *value summits* to make sure the organization's values are still reflective of what's in people's hearts.

To me, culture has always been a bit like an iceberg. It's easier to see the things above the waterline: policies, strategy, and product development. It's much harder to see what lies below—the long-held beliefs, assumptions, and unconscious biases. Unfortunately, leaders haven't been doing a great job at working below the waterline. A study carried out by Deloitte revealed that while great stock is being placed on culture to drive growth, only 28% of employees believed they understood their culture well and a scant 18% believed their organization had the "right" culture.[51]

Even more shocking, a mere 9% of organizations reported they were able to initiate a culture change despite their best efforts. At times like these, leaders need to take the icy plunge to explore the unwritten rules and behaviours that are holding the organization back. Initiatives like those developed at Unilever are a great start to helping employees cocreate an aligned culture founded on values and collective purpose.

The litmus test to determine whether you have a strong culture is to ask employees whether they feel they are being treated fairly and whether they feel that they are free to speak truth to power. Anonymous engagement surveys or suggestion boxes are an obvious path forward. But there's a problem here: I can't tell you how many employee engagement surveys I've seen collecting either digital or physical dust. They're locked away in some file because the results are so poor that no one wants to share them. Leaders don't know where to begin. Be courageous by reviewing those scores and working cooperatively with your colleagues to say, "What are the two or three most critical pieces to move the dial on? Where is the low-hanging fruit?" Think hard about what you plan to do with the responses before you send out a survey. Who should see what information first? How will you ensure frontline workers know that you have heard them? How will the C-suite implement the changes to maximize impact?

Make it clear that responses will be closely read, evaluated, and shared. In a lot of human resources assignments we work on, we've moved away from laying out the traditional employee engagement road map with complicated lines, arrows, and boxes. Now we find our clients better served by designing a "GPS map," where we deliver step-by-step directions to reach their destination. This framework enables us to more quickly synthesize and identify short-, medium-, and long-term goals and targets. Taking these steps makes employees feel heard. But remember: being heard isn't enough. Teams want to not only see action, but also be a part of the action, once the results are in.

THE DANGERS OF DISTANCING

As we've just seen, holding information back from employees negatively affects culture. This classic form of distancing quickly erodes trust. This section explores four major types of distancing that affect morale and goodwill: structural, physical, social, and cultural. While it's not always intentional, leaders sometimes underestimate the dangers that distancing creates between peers, teams, departments, and networks.[52]

Structural distancing sees leaders using organizational charts, rules, and protocols as a crutch to distance themselves from their employees. Higher-ups may put gatekeepers in place, who create barriers to easy and transparent access by employees. Be mindful of your organization's structure, and make sure people know how to get a hold of you when they need to share important information. The rise of whistleblower policies is an example of organizations helping employees come forward to get the right information into the right people's hands.

With *physical distancing*, leaders may be floors—or miles—away from the people they work with. As we learned during the pandemic, mandated physical distancing demanded an entirely new set of leadership capabilities. More than ever, leaders need to have a full appreciation of what's happening via screen. There are reams of information these days on how to use virtual meetings more effectively. Cocreate protocols with your team: many teams have instituted policies where everyone agrees, for example, to have their cameras turned on. Prepare for these meetings with a well-thought-out agenda and give people time for breaks to recharge the batteries as much as to socialize with one another. For those leaders who may have introverts on the team, call them ahead of the meeting and let them know if you will be calling on them to make a contribution.

Social distancing happens as people rise to more senior ranks and they begin to both separate and align themselves by belonging to formal groups like the C-suite or informal groups such as ad hoc committees or special clubs. "Proximity" to power—sometimes expressed in terms like "mahogany row," "headquarters," or the "penthouse suite"—should not be underestimated. Many in these groups see the information they carry as more credible and authoritative than those below them. We see "circling of wagons" as leaders align themselves to the dominant way of thinking of the moment,[53] leaving teams to work behind the scenes to adapt their behaviour to an ever-changing rebalancing of power. To reduce social distancing, many organizations are simply doing away altogether with clustering C-suite offices on remote floors. Nowadays, you'll see the chief human resources officer or chief financial officer embedded with their team. This dramatically improves communication among team members as well as sending a signal that the department is open and listening.

Cultural distancing occurs when leaders favour certain individuals and teams and alienate others. This creates "inside" and "outside" groups. By dividing groups and playing favourites, teams become more deferential in order to curry favour. People feel that in order to preserve their jobs, they need to bow and scrape to higher-ups. The fallout from this form of distancing sees the erosion of cultural pride, innovation, trust, and loyalty. My mother used to advise me to "consider the source." Next time someone approaches you, ask yourself, Why are they sharing this information with me now? What are they hoping to gain? What are they expecting me to do with it? They may be setting you up, perhaps manipulating you, or worse still, dividing and conquering you and your peers.

There are many ways to reduce the challenges of distancing. The first is simply to be aware of what they are, be on the lookout for them, and develop specific plans to avoid or minimize them. Kurt Lewin's three-step process offers a good framework: first "unfreeze" a specific area of culture you want to work on. This might be addressing how conflict is dealt with or how decisions are made. By deliberately opening up one area of focus, you will have a better chance of success. Next comes the tricky bit: while working through this period of ambiguity, you want to start cocreating and codifying the new conditions that will govern the future behaviour as well as updating policies and procedures. And finally, once this phase is complete, you want to "refreeze" by communicating the new norms.[54] By regularly undertaking this work, you will be constantly refreshing and transforming culture.

BE CAPABLE, BE CREDIBLE, BE TRANSPARENT

You have learned a lot in this chapter about the importance of building trust in an organization and about the ways that trust impacts employee retention and a company's financial performance. But how do you build the skills to grow trust in your own team?

There are three major attributes leaders can develop to strengthen team alignment and accountability. The first: employees are looking for capable leaders, so you need to become one. How often have we heard grumblings about someone new coming into a leadership role who may be "the favourite" but is perhaps not fully equipped to handle the job? If that just happens to be you, know that you are being sized up from day one on your expertise, knowledge, and experience. Of course, we can't know everything, but it's important to have humility, admit what you don't know, and close those gaps as quickly as possible. Show people that you are a rapid learner and a quick study. This goes a long way to closing the trust gap.

Next up: character. A culture can quickly sour when its leaders— and team members—have significant character flaws. Organizations are looking for leaders of impeccable character, people who do what they say they will do and keep their promises. To turn negative situations around, you must model the behaviour you wish to see. Be that person who is always thinking of others and who has their backs. People on the receiving end of your good graces will begin to emulate them. Equally, leaders need to be regarded as people who are reliable, committed to following through, and able to successfully get a project over the finish line. And if there are people on your team who lack credibility, don't deliver when they say they will, or can't be trusted with information, you have a big coaching opportunity to help them improve their character too.

Finally, you must be a superlative communicator who clearly and frequently delivers honest feedback, news, and information that is trustworthy. Nothing will hurt a healthy team culture faster than malicious rumours filled with misinformation, or just plain gossip. I remember working in an organization where the rumour mill was running over time about a person whose performance was slipping. People were eagerly speculating that they had a drinking problem, were lazy, in over their head—all the usual comments one might hear in the coffee room. Turns out, this person was trying to look after an aging parent with dementia and had just found out their partner had been unfaithful. Now who looks foolish and untrustworthy?

As a leader, as soon as you even glean a hint or trace of rumours or gossip, you need to shut them down. Be the bloodhound who sniffs out the source of the information, and then confront those spreading rumours.

Fulfill on those three fronts—capability, character, and communication—and you will see the team trust barometer steadily rising.

OUR STORIES ARE OUR CULTURE

Stories are powerful. The best ones represent an organization's culture, giving colour to its abstract principles and values. They can be the best kind of teacher. They can also be your canary in the coal mine. The stories that evolve over time in your organization are both a direct reflection of your current culture and an influence on how the culture evolves. If we go back to our examples of Better.com and Unilever, think about the kind of stories that might have been circulating. Internally, Better.com's story might have been negatively dubbed "Worse.com," and as we know, this story would travel far beyond the physical and virtual walls of the place. On the other hand, Unilever's positive story might have been called "Lever for Change" because of all the work underway to support global issues. Stories speak volumes about what the organization stands for. These are the stories that end up on social media platforms and review sites like Glassdoor.com.

Often when we tell or hear the stories in our own organizations, we laugh, shrug, and say, "That's just the way things are around here." Relational leaders don't accept that. They are always on the lookout for stories that celebrate success and positivity while being vigilant to ferret out stories that spread negativity and fear. These leaders facilitate the development of new stories. Stories are one of the best ways to introduce changes to culture because they appeal to the widest possible breadth of learning styles, accelerate learning, and jog our memory better than any data set ever will.[55] Well-crafted tales help us form a moral to the story that guides future actions. Stories have the power to change work rituals and positively affect the day-to-day rhythms of a place.

Microsoft is an interesting case study in how stories nurture culture and rebuild trust. When Satya Nadella first started in his new role as Microsoft's CEO, their story was a demoralizing one. After ten years of Steve Ballmer's command-and-control leadership, people were exhausted and fearful. The root cause of this was a system Ballmer had instituted called "stack rating," where every member of the company was judged relative to their peers. If you worked in a group of ten, two peers would get great ratings, six would get a pass, and two would fail. It didn't matter how brilliant you were or how much money you brought into the company; someone always had to be ranked at the bottom.

The "stack ranking" story became legendary at Microsoft and profoundly affected the way people worked together. It fostered competition rather than collaboration, and Microsoft superstars did not want to work with their peers for fear of being killed in the rankings. As a result, a culture that was once curious and intensely research driven turned inward on itself. Employees just didn't see Microsoft as "cool" anymore, saying they saw it as "technology's answer to Sears"[56]—and we all know what happened to Sears.

And then along came Nadella. He immediately got to work soliciting new stories from every corner of the company—stories that would restore pride to employees. He also put out his own narrative. Embodying the organization's new ethos, Nadella said, "If you want to be cool, go elsewhere. But if you want to join a company that is committed to making others cool, join Microsoft."[57]

His sentiment reflects the principles of relational leadership. It speaks to a dedication to appreciating others, embracing new ways to see context, designing new processes to share stories, and mobilizing collective team intelligence. Microsoft achieved this by harnessing relational leadership's underpinning value proposition: *everyone is leading all the time.* As they led Microsoft, employees were newly empowered to make customer-centric decisions, generating clarity and energy to "future-proof" the organization.

It was Nadella's commitment to relational leadership that helped Microsoft get back in the game. As you contemplate your next opportunity to nurture culture, consider how stories have the power to *hold us* and *move us*. What do I mean by this? Well-worn stories *hold us* firmly in place to honour history, build legacy, and uphold ethics. New stories *move us* to question assumptions. We need both these kinds of stories. As a relational leader, you are the glue that holds the stories of the past and the present in tandem. By doing this, you'll ignite new stories that will continue to shape organizational culture.

You'll know you've been successful in creating stories that change culture when you walk down the hall one day and hear a story you helped shape being told by someone else who is treating it as *their own*. That's a good day. When these stories go viral, they galvanize commitment, grow loyalty, and, importantly, build trust.

According to experts, the stories floating around our organizations are one of the most important ways employees learn about and model the culture. If you have a healthy culture, that's great. But what if you have a toxic culture?

I once had an assignment in an organization where everyone yelled at each other. I was told the behaviour started after a new leader joined. The story circulating was that if you wanted anything to get done, you yelled just like the VP did. The "yelling story" gave people permission to copycat this negative behaviour.

Now consider my own story of "earned and granted trust." As a new employee, I was told by the CEO that I had to "earn" their trust. So what did I do? I worked like a dog, observing their behaviour, mimicking their every move. The CEO was a workaholic, so I became a workaholic. Leaving at seven thirty on a Friday night, I was often asked if I was "working a half day." The CEO insisted that every decision be reviewed by them first, meaning I was gathering insane amounts of data to make a case and constantly second-guessing myself. Ultimately, I left that organization and joined another. On the first day of that job, the CEO said to me, "I trust you today, I trust you right now. I have your back." They had given me "granted" trust. The difference, as you can imagine, between "earned" trust and "granted" trust was incredible. Without being micromanaged or second-guessed, I felt free to do the work I was hired to do. I have told this story many times in many different forums because it reaffirms how polarizing leadership behaviours affect the cultural values of an organization.

As I have learned working with organizations, there are a number of different kinds of stories that can help nurture culture. One of my favourites is the "elephant in the room story," which helps teams identify dysfunction and how to meet it head-on. The "purpose story" helps rally people around a cause. The "leap story" supports leaders in laying out a vision for future strategy. The "dangerous expert story" prepares leaders for enterprise-wide initiatives by arming them with key questions to ensure strong execution. Having a number of stories like these at your fingertips will help you begin to transform culture.

WHAT YOU CAN LEARN ABOUT CULTURE FROM THE FOO FIGHTERS

To illustrate how employees and leaders come together to shape culture, let's look at a story I've dubbed the "story of the houselights," which comes from none other than Dave Grohl, founder of the Foo Fighters, who has an interesting take on what it means to nurture culture.

In May 2020, Dave wrote a story in *The Atlantic* about how he was coping with the pandemic.[58] Within this story, he told another one that stopped me in my tracks. Perhaps unintentionally—though you never know with Dave—he described to a T a leader's role in nurturing culture.

Dave started off by sharing how important the power of intimacy is in performance and how much he missed it. That led him to share a story about a choice that U2 made on their *Elevation* tour in 2000. He described how the band simply walked on stage, houselights on full, without the usual cue of darkness followed by flashing videos and lasers. He talked about the shock the audience felt in not being cloaked in dark isolation, of not being treated to a grand entrance: "This was no accident . . . It was a lesson in intimacy." Remarkably, this surprise effect shrank the size of the stadium to a "dirty nightclub at last call, every blemish in view."

That concert could have been just like all the others—an anonymous black pit, its floor filled with rolling beer cans (never wear suede boots to an arena concert). But a game-changing choice put power in *everyone's* hands. That night, it was up to the audience, as much as the band, to define what their newly emerging culture would look and feel like—right then and there.

There are a number of lessons we can take from Dave's story. The first is that leaders need to *develop intimacy*. They also need to size up the situation and *be daring enough to experiment with any "business as usual" expectations* that employees may have. Deliberately setting out to disrupt is jarring and uncomfortable; it may stretch people beyond their usual risk tolerance. But it's these moments that ignite cultural change. As U2 walked out into a fully lit arena, it kept its promise to fans as a band that continually stretches its creative limits. They were OK with putting themselves on trial. This is what you sign up for if you become a leader. Like those who attended the concert, every day we want to feel that we are part of something special, progressive, and ever changing. We might try to describe our workplace to someone who doesn't work there, but that person wouldn't *get it*. They hadn't been there to cocreate it. This is a hallmark of a great story and a strong culture—it can't be replicated.

Another lesson is that just as fast as we destabilize the environment, we need to *create smooth interfaces* between the world that was and the new one that is forming. This goes back to Kurt Lewin's three-step model of unfreezing, dealing with ambiguity, and refreezing. Think about the shock most fans would have experienced as they searched each other's eyes trying to gauge reactions. You can imagine that eyebrows-up look: "Is this for real?" But along the way they cocreated group affirmation. Like those Microsoft employees, they now had "cool factor," contributing to something very different and special. In that first defining moment, the audience might have felt cheated, but as the vibe spread they would have felt that the band made the right decision. And with that, the band *gained* trust through what was a pretty audacious move. The audience then relaxed. They were in the right place, with the right people—their people. U2 placed their audience at the very centre of an exciting experiment and asked them to take a leap of faith. A moment of singular alignment. They walked out exhausted but not feeling tired. Exhilarated and creative. They wanted more.

Is that how you and your team feel when you leave work at night? You should.

CREATING "WE" STORIES

Now that we've examined how to develop cultural intimacy, let's review stories from Wendy Zatylny, whom we met earlier, and David Goldstein, CEO of Travel Alberta. Wendy describes a moment of truth she experienced while leading a communications team at the Summit of the Americas in 2001, while David talks about a leadership practice he used when he arrived at Destination Canada. In Wendy's story we witness the forming of a culture, built around the trust that a complete group of strangers gave each other as they faced a crisis together. David's story highlights how a new leader builds trust in an organization that is well established and may be stuck in their ways.

> Wendy: I took on trying to manage something I had very little experience in. I learned just before the summit that my counterpart, responsible for the technical aspects, was let go. I talked to my boss and said, "OK, give it to me." And as we got into things, I learned that activists were threatening to take down websites. I convened a meeting of all the technical people—none of whom I'd ever met.
>
> So, I've got all these people, and I sit them down in a room, and I'm so not a techie! I laid out a goal for the meeting; I said, "This is the desired outcome." I need a process to come out of this meeting. I had to focus on the process and the outcome. It was the weirdest thing: for the first time, and probably the only time in my life, I actively chaired a meeting in which I really didn't understand the content, nor a lot of technical aspects of the discussion.
>
> Jill: How did it unfold?
>
> Wendy: I just focused on the process and on the outcome. I let them work out the details, but I made

sure by the end of the meeting we had an agreed-upon
process pathway, reporting and accountability strategy, and timeline. And it was brilliant! We came under
multiple intense cyber-attacks. We were the only site
not to go down. We had so much redundancy built in,
our servers never broke a sweat. All the bigger players
went down; they all got hacked and went offline. We
just kept chugging along. We became a best-practice
template, and I did it without even knowing what I was
doing.

In Wendy's story we see an example of where strong facilitation
meets confident vulnerability. This "courage under fire" moment tested
her ability to create an empowered culture with a team who barely
knew each other. As we trace her process, we see a few things at work:
she set out a desired outcome (not to get hacked); facilitated a meeting
to set out the process to achieve that outcome (freeing the experts to
determine what needed to be done to achieve it); and she established
structure (by introducing communication protocols, accountabilities,
and timelines).

She created a culture of trust with a singular focus, one in which
the expertise of each team member was acknowledged. And she did all
this lacking experience in the specifics, demonstrating the relational
leadership capability of leading goal-oriented discussions that inspire
the alignment and accountability to drive team innovation. That day,
Wendy became a "dangerous expert." The next time you gather your
team together in a high-pressure situation, remember Wendy.

When David Goldstein became CEO of Destination Canada,
he used a technique he called *diagnostique* to unlock resistance to
new ideas and assuage suspicions of an outsider coming in to shake
things up.

David: We started changing the culture. We said
goodbye to some people and we hired some people
from the private sector. And the other thing I did was
to approach the people who remained and ask them
if they would move to different positions around the

table. They really flourished. They were ready for it. I found three or four people from the senior management group and asked them to try doing different things. And just by shifting their seat, it gave them a different perspective.

It may be one of the smallest things I did, but it may go down as one of the most critical things I did. What's interesting now is when I canvass my leadership team, the two biggest skeptics are now some of my biggest supporters.

Jill: How did you change their minds?

David: I spent time with each of them and then collectively we developed a real mission statement, not something written on a whiteboard somewhere. I showed them I was open to new ideas, and I wasn't just in it for change for the sake of change. I shared my mantra with them: "There's no change for the sake of change, but there's no the same for the sake of the same."

Jill: How did you create that new mission statement?

David: This is what I learned from Mike McCabe.* I created my own *Future Plan*. I walked everyone through a process by asking questions: Why are we here? What business are we in? The breakthrough occurred when I asked, "Who is the real customer?"

It's not a traveller. That's what everyone thought. I said, "We need to become a media company." We all came to the same conclusion, that the customer is not the audience; it's the advertiser, the subscriber. We had to stop thinking about marketing to individual travellers. Our job was to define the right audiences and

---

* Michael McCabe was CEO of the Canadian Association of Broadcasters from 1988 to 2001. David recalls using what Michael called *diagnostique* to draft CAB's two strategic plans, "Taking the Lead" and "Future Plan." He is recognized as a leader in positioning broadcasting as a vital component supporting Canada's cultural objectives. Michael passed away in 2020 while working in Vietnam.

deliver them to the Canadian industry. That was a fundamental shift. A lot of light bulbs went on.

Jill: So, you turned the model on its head. How did you come to that conclusion?

David: I surrounded myself with people smarter than me and I'm a great diagnostician; I may suck at everything else, but that's another thing I learned from Michael. It's like the difference between a great GP and a great specialist. A really great GP is a really good diagnostician. And I remember what McCabe taught us to use—the *diagnostique*—spell check doesn't even like that word.

Does vision shape culture or does culture shape vision? The answer, of course, is that each shapes the other. At the heart of David's story, we see how being patient, being open to leading tough conversations, and working collaboratively created a radically transformed vision. Significantly, it was a story from David's past, the story of *diagnostique*, that inspired him to be a generalist, not a specialist. An important lesson for all leaders as they take on increasing responsibilities.

PRACTICE NURTURING CULTURE

Here's my seven-step practice you can use to nurture culture and build trust:

- **Step 1: Listen to workplace stories.** What's circulating out there? As you begin a culture-changing exercise, conduct an audit of stories now circulating. Begin by asking open-ended questions like "How are things going on your end?" Then move on to ask questions focusing on specific issues. Give people plenty of time to elaborate; ask them to explain how things are working—or not working. Summarize what you're hearing. Ask questions like "Does that sound right? Am I missing anything?" and encourage people to fill in the gaps.

- **Step 2: Interpret what the stories are saying.** Use this checklist to document what you think the story says about your organization:
  - Who's telling the story and how far has it circulated?
  - What is the story saying about how work gets done and how leaders behave?
  - What existing cultural norms and behaviours are revealed in the story?
  - What are people saying about the story? Do they believe it's true?
  - What does the story say about relationships between departments?
  - What operational policies are either supporting or failing employees?
  - How do your organization's physical workspaces and offices play into the story?
  - What does the story say about hierarchy and unwritten rules?
  - What role is social media playing in amplifying the story?
  - Where in the organization are you seeing positive stories?
  - What are those departments doing differently than other areas of the company?

- **Step 3: Involve everyone.** Tap into the insights of team members, and ask them to describe obstacles, barriers, bottlenecks, or where red tape exists. Go from department to department to find the storytellers, and encourage them to share stories of strength. Look for similarities and differences.

- **Step 4: Become a better communicator and a master storyteller.** Many employees say there's not enough concrete information about action to be taken once a process in cultural change begins. Use the GPS method we talked about earlier, map out a step-by-step process, and encourage feedback. Know your organization inside and out so that you can connect stories across departments; work with your peers to create shared storylines; host forums to share innovative stories you hear from outside your organization; and use stories as examples to demonstrate the kinds of change the company is seeking. Spread the story.

- **Step 5: Deputize cultural ambassadors.** Be on the lookout for pockets of innovation where great stories live, and develop relationships with the holders of the stories. Ask them to make the rounds with you to share their story—they can become your biggest allies.

- **Step 6: Provide rewards and recognition.** Share your great stories with senior leaders, and make sure your team has an opportunity to present them and bask in the moment. Hold company forums, host lunch-and-learns, use social media and industry conferences to share the stories broadly.

- **Step 7: Continually replenish the story bank.** Stories get tired. Be constantly on the lookout to unearth new stories. You're just as likely to find them during a casual hallway conversation as you are at your next strategic off-site.

Evaluate Your Performance

To kick-start your new practices and behaviours, reflect on these questions to consider how your values mesh with your organization's culture and its stories.

- How do you instill trust in the people you work with?

_____

_____

_____

- When you think about the building blocks to develop trust—being capable, credible, and transparent—which do you feel you need to work on the most?

_____

_____

_____

- What's a word or phrase that describes your *current* culture?

_____

_____

_____

- What's a word or phrase that describes the culture you would like to see in the future?

  _____

  _____

  _____

- Think of a story currently circulating around your office. What does it say about your culture?

  _____

  _____

  _____

- How well are you doing at fostering teamwork that is both interdependent and independent?

  _____

  _____

  _____

- If you could change one thing in your culture right now, what would it be?

  _____

  _____

  _____

- What kinds of stories would be needed to begin this change?

_____

_____

_____

- Where in your organization can you find a story that signals the kind of culture the organization wishes to nurture?

_____

_____

_____

CHAPTER 6

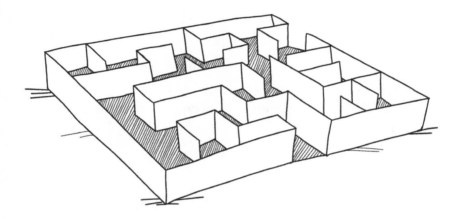

Practice Navigating Complexity

When you hit a wrong note, it's the next note that
makes it good or bad.
—*Miles Davis, trumpeter, band leader, composer*

We all hit a wrong note now and again.

Herbie Hancock recalled just such a moment in the 1960s when
he was playing with the great trumpeter Miles Davis: "It was a really
hot night. The music was on. Right in the middle of Miles's solo, when
he was playing one of his amazing solos, I played the wrong chord.
Completely wrong. It sounded like a big mistake. And Miles paused for
a second. And then he played some notes that made my chord right,
that made it correct. Miles didn't hear a mistake, he heard it as something that happened. An event. And so that was part of the reality of

what was happening at that moment. And he dealt with it. Since he didn't hear it as a mistake, he felt it was his responsibility to find something that fit. That taught me a very big lesson, about not only music but about life."[59]

This pearl of wisdom tells us that the key to becoming a successful navigator is in how we respond. For leaders, it's not about *not* making mistakes; it's about how we recover, what we learn, and how we pass that knowledge on to others.

Let's take a look at what went terribly wrong for WeWork CEO Adam Neumann.

In 2019, Adam was ousted from WeWork, the company he built, which at the time was valued at $47 billion. At first blush, this is a head-scratcher. How could someone who revolutionized coworking office space, growing the company to eight hundred global locations, be forced out? The story that emerged a few weeks later told the tale: Neumann not only had stopped listening; he had become tone-deaf, an attribute we saw in the *asshole syndrome*—one of the seven deadly derailers.

This misfire caused his stellar career to end with a thud. Reflecting on his downfall, Adam recalled a moment of truth when he squandered a rare opportunity to benefit from the wisdom of Apple CEO Tim Cook. Adam admitted that during their ninety-minute sit-down, he talked almost the whole time rather than listened. The power had gone to his head, causing him to lose focus on his core business and its vision.[60] He lost sight of the fact that his team was trying to tell him the company was in trouble. When WeWork's value went into a free fall, plunging from $47 billion to $10 billion, Adam acknowledged he'd become "less adept at seeing things from other people's point of view."[61]

WHAT'S AT STAKE

The cost of workplace mistakes and missteps is far-reaching, dragging down organizational performance as much as reputation. A KPMG study found that despite best intentions, only 19% of organizations deliver successful projects and only 44% meet their original goals and business intent.[62] More telling, though, the study revealed that it's a leader's inability to quickly read changing dynamics, shift priorities, and change their behaviour that dooms them. Recognizing the types of people and kind of events that push your buttons will help you from making rash decisions that you'll regret later. But simply recognizing knee-jerk reactions isn't enough; practicing that critical reflexivity we talked about earlier will help you uncover the root cause of why these things upset you. Once uncovered, the next step is to tame those first impulses to act and work to create new behaviours.

NAVIGATE COMPLEXITY: LEARN FROM YOUR MISTAKES

How do you make the most of your mistakes? The trick is learning how to become a stronger navigator and teaching yourself new behaviours to interpret multiple perspectives more quickly. Remember back in the first practice when we talked about reflexivity as the new yoga? Think of this chapter's practice as a new form of leadership Pilates, further strengthening your core.

We make all kinds of missteps every day. Maybe it's a bad hire or a failed strategic initiative, or we become embroiled in internecine politics. Whatever it may be, you know that feeling—you're in the middle of what I call the "messy maze" and you can't find your way out. We're all familiar with the symptoms, which range from sleepless nights to short tempers. The costs can be high, as decisions and choices we make affect our professional and personal lives, reputation, and well-being. Assessing and improving how we navigate through tough circumstances helps us prevent repeating them.

Think about a big project you might have recently taken on. Remember the hope, energy, and "can-do" attitude everyone had as you set out? Now think back to the ending, when you achieved your goal. Remember savouring that sweet moment of success? Now what about the middle? It's a fog. Anyone who has led a complex project will tell you that the middle of a project is a swamp, where we are tested, in some cases, to the very limits of our character, experience, and patience.

During the 2009 economic downturn, Harvard professor Rosabeth Moss Kanter sensitized us to the need to adopt new practices when we find ourselves in these predicaments. Exhorting leaders to embrace Kanter's Law, she told them to buck up: "Everything looks like a failure in the middle. Everyone loves inspired beginnings and happy endings; it is just the middles that involve hard work."[63] Her insights received a lot of attention, and she went on to coin the phrase "the messy middle," encouraging people to develop persistence and perseverance as they wade through the tortuous paths of "middleness." Up to this point, many leaders intuitively felt the pain of the middle, but until Kanter put a name to it, they didn't have a way to put their finger on the source of their angst.

Kanter suggests organizations take three actions to break this spell. The first is to set the right tone at the top, harnessing strong communications that keep the mission clear. The second is to strike rapid improvement teams to adjust and fix operations. The third is where many falter: remembering to focus on the long term. With so many demands, leaders struggle to make time to view things with a longer lens. Kanter urges leaders to launch future-oriented initiatives in tandem with immediate crises to combat our tendency to lose site of the endgame.

HOW DO YOU KNOW YOU'RE IN THE MAZE?

The crucial step is to know you've got a problem. Sometimes it's glaringly obvious. Many times, you won't necessarily know the root cause of the problem, but you can certainly see (and feel) the symptoms. Relational leaders need to be on the lookout for the signs that something is amiss. You'll know you're in the middle of the maze when you experience or witness one or more of the following symptoms:

- You're experiencing doubt or fear or questioning your competence to carry through.
- Communications break down throughout the team.
- The big picture is lost in translation.
- It's increasingly difficult to connect the dots.
- One view dominates.
- Fractured views stifle alignment.

- More mistakes are being made as the project moves along.
- People cover up mistakes and/or withhold information.
- People and situations are misjudged.
- Assumptions are made.
- Problems arise that weren't anticipated.
- The project encounters repeated "near misses," whereby it risks becoming seriously derailed.
- The team is demoralized, paralyzed, and unable to move forward.
- There's no end in sight.

If any of these are feeling all too familiar, it's time to get to work and guide the team out of the messy maze.

NAVIGATING THE MAZE

When I think about how leaders can better navigate messy projects, I like to use the analogy of a maze. Imagine entering a maze on a sunny fall day. As we take those first few steps, we feel excitement and the energy to "conquer" it. We are at ease, feeling competent. Pretty soon, those positive sentiments give way to feeling perplexed and impatient. What began as a fun activity turns into a taxing obstacle course. We should have gone left but took a right turn instead. We end up down a blind alley or find ourselves in a dizzying roundabout and become more disoriented. We're in the middle of the maze.

The first thing we need to do is to go back to our old practice of taking a pause. While your first inclination may be to keep going at all costs, it's vital that you check yourself when you begin to realize you're in a jam. Pausing helps us to mentally *retrace our steps and evaluate how we got here.* It's here that you need to take stock. Take a hard look at your own behaviour. Ask yourself how you are supporting those around you. Review decisions taken and the criteria under which they were made.

At this stage, we may find different people trying to take charge of the group and deciding where to go next. Frayed nerves jangle; the group may snap at each other as they come upon yet another dead end. Advice that was once encouraged is now not even sought. Muted silence hangs over the group. People may start to blame each other, asking, "Whose idea was it to visit this maze in the first place?" Trust erodes as the suggestions of others turn out to be just one more bum steer. Some members of the group may decide to go it on their own, believing their instincts to be superior. A dark cloud moves in as people feel lost, fatigued, stressed, and grumpy. When we're at this phase, we've got to *help the team reconnect, encourage debate, hear concerns, rest fears, and reenergize the group.*

Leaders need to find and optimize the common unifying thread: everyone wants to get out of the maze. As a leader, our job is to *open up* and *focus* the path and to be positive and purposeful. No matter how bleak things may look, we need to ensure the team never loses sight of the end, never gives up on each other. These moments of angst are dividing lines—they separate out leaders who know how to rise to the occasion from those who wander around in circles. It's in these moments that we need to *manage emotions and watch out for automatic behaviour*—both ours and the team's—that may prevent us from seeing things from each other's perspectives. Encouraging everyone to speak up and share ideas needs to be balanced with creating a unified plan to move forward. That's where your cooler head needs to prevail.

Remember in our last practice we developed stories to nurture trust and build team strength? This is a good time to *share a story* of when you've been in this place before. By sharing your "messy maze" story—warts and all—you'll accomplish three things: You'll put people at ease (hey, we've been here before), give them hope (we can get through this together), and encourage new behaviours (let's try something new and different to get out of here).

It's up to leaders to *coach the team to be both autonomous and interdependent.* Ask the group to identify roadblocks or obstacles. Find out where knowledge gaps exist, and work to close them. Bring in experts who have different experiences to share. Create a climate where it's OK to talk about fuckups. Acknowledging these helps the team recover by talking through what went right and what went wrong. Even the best people make errors; a relational leader accepts them and helps everyone learn from them. Your work is to harvest the best out of these broader perspectives. Measure the possible outcomes of starting again, retracing your steps, or going off in a completely different direction. But let's be clear: once you've heard the options, it's up to you to summon all your knowledge and experience to decide the best course of action. These will be some of your loneliest moments. That's why having a series of steps to process your way through the messy maze is so vital.

We're never going to prevent every misstep or mistake, but having this practice on hand will help you navigate eventualities and ensure that the mistakes don't derail the project altogether. And if you handle it well, you've just created a teachable moment, a great story that will contribute to strengthening culture and developing practices to learn more deeply and quickly.

ONE LEADER'S JOURNEY NAVIGATING THE MAZE

In my interview with Jonathan Kay, I asked him to reflect on leading during difficult times. As we sipped our coffee, he reflected on his early days of becoming the editor in chief of *The Walrus*, and he shared with me: "If you're not constantly asking the question 'What does it all mean?' you're not a leader. I convinced myself, I'm good at leading. I thought, I was successful at my old job, I'll be successful in this job."

Jon left his role as editor in chief of the *National Post* to helm the national magazine in 2014, where he inherited a team whom he described as living in three camps: one camp had their arms open; they were eager and happy he'd arrived. The second camp crossed their arms, challenging his leadership. They were simply waiting him out— what I call those who "quit but stayed." The third had their hands on their hips, waiting to see what he would do. Looking back, Jonathan reflected: "I came in and treated everyone like they had their hands on their hips."

THE TALE OF TWO WALRUSES

The long shadow cast by *The Walrus*'s highly regarded publisher,

Shelley Ambrose, caused further challenges. Shelley had saved the organization from bankruptcy, and her vision of the magazine and Jon's clashed as they began to work together. Jon shared, "We had weekly management meetings, and I said, 'There's two *Walrus*es. There's the *Walrus* I'm creating, with editorial and investigative journalism and spicy stuff and then there's these *Walrus* Talks.'" The way Jon saw it, the publisher liked the idea of *The Walrus* as a "travelling corporate-funded cocktail party" rather than the hard-hitting journalism he had come to know at the *National Post*. Jonathan drew a line in the sand, telling her, "You need to make a decision about this organization." He said, "If my ego hadn't got in the way, I would have quit six months earlier. At the end of the day, it was either my vision or this other vision. It became increasingly clear that I wasn't going to win. I had no interest in that."

Reflecting on this tumultuous time, Jonathan said, "A huge component of leadership is ego suppression—there's so many instances where transitions occur and the person who's leading says, 'I created this.'" Jon found himself straddling two worlds: the one that had been in existence since Shelley arrived and the one that he thought he'd been hired to create. It was clear as their meetings unfolded that the dynamic rainmaker, who had saved the organization, felt they knew the best path forward. Jon had the feeling that, until he had arrived, the organization had hired people who didn't challenge or say no to Shelley.

Jonathan's story is an example of how complicated it can be to take on new roles with increasing responsibility, especially if you are given a mandate to "create change." Rarely is the job you sign up for the job you take on. You want to be as prepared as you can be to navigate the politics, power, and personalities that factor into every aspect of a job. As we see in Jonathan's case, one of the toughest challenges is to strike a balance between acknowledging legacy and anchoring new vision— as well as bringing people along with you as you implement change.

If you were in Jonathan's shoes, what would you have done differently? One thing I've learned is that you can never do enough homework when you are being recruited for a new role. As much as headhunters and selection committees are interviewing you, you need to be interviewing *them*. Remember our conversation in chapter 2 when we talked about listening to your inner voice? Here was Jonathan's moment: "I remember he [a board member] gave a speech once at a *Walrus* gala and he basically said, 'My wife says this is a worthy orga- nization. Then I wrote a cheque, and that's why I'm here.' When I met him after I joined and spoke about this divide between publishing and editorial, he said to me, 'What did you expect?' And he was right." At the time, Jonathan thought little of it, but when he looked back, he re- alized it was a defining moment—one that was telling him something wasn't right.

Whether you're meeting the chair of the board or the CEO for the first time, study their background; assess them as coolly as they are evaluating you. Arm yourself with good questions to ask. Gauge body language and reactions as people respond to your inquiries. I remem- ber in one CEO position I was interviewing for, I asked the selection committee (composed of board members), "What's your vision for this organization?" A pretty simple question, right? At that moment, I could see some board members staring at each other. Others had their eyes downcast. There was a chill in the air, and people looked uncom- fortable. I had found a place of vulnerability. But just like Jonathan, I ignored it. I put on my superwoman cape and thought I could "save" the place. What a mistake that was.

Finally, while it may seem obvious, you need to drill into your fu- ture organization's finances. I am continually surprised by candidates who have had only a cursory look at the books and have failed to ask questions. If you are sensing hesitancy around sharing financial in- formation, run for the hills. If you are not as competent in this area as you need to be, enlist help, start taking courses, or find a mentor. Dig like a ferret into past annual reports, research online, and reach out to colleagues who may have an insider's view of what's really going on.

PEER COACHING HELPS MAKE SENSE OF THINGS

Usually the more complex the problem, the higher the stakes. And the higher the stakes, the more things there are to go wrong. I remember working with a large telecommunications firm whose leaders managed projects worth hundreds of millions. I was impressed by how they epitomized grace under pressure. How did they do it? They established peer learning circles to troubleshoot, bounce ideas off each other, and give each other support. In addition to there being regular meetings, anyone could convene a meeting at any time. There was a common understanding that when someone asked for a meeting, they needed help.

To *develop your peer learning circle*, follow these simple principles: establish a time that works for everyone and commit to showing up. Set up a standard structure using questions like:

- What key challenge or question are you up against?
- How might others view this situation?
- What future are you trying to create?
- What do you need to let go of, and what do you need to learn?
- Where do you need input or help?
- What images, metaphors, feelings, and gestures capture what you've heard?
- What step or experiment could you try to set you on your journey?[64]

Periodically evaluate your progress as a peer learning group to ensure everyone is benefiting; discuss what is working well or not well.

As we saw in our maze example, project managers need to be experts in one of the most important stances in leadership Pilates: pause, plan, and prepare. I know, I know, it seems counterintuitive. Typically, when we find ourselves in a jam, the first thing a leader wants to do is to dive into a flurry of action. But take my advice. *Gain some distance on your problem first.* I'm not talking about taking a month off and running away to Hawaii. When you find yourself spinning, get up, take a walk, get outside for fresh air, grab a coffee. This will keep you from doing something rash, saying something you might regret later, or having a complete meltdown in the middle of the office. Trust me. I've been there and done all three (although not at the same time . . .).

Next, *reach out.* Call up a trusted friend, talk to your partner, or engage a mentor or coach. It's vital to have an outlet for your feelings, talk things out, and reason things through. Do these things *before* you have a heart-to-heart with the boss. Use our powerful reflective tool, rehearsal, to help you clarify and practice next steps. Have mock con-versations, do scenario planning, draft out a risk mitigation register—maybe you need to do all three. The most important thing is keeping chaos and panic at bay. This is a time to be methodical, clearheaded, and focused.

Then *document what has happened* so that you can reflect on it later. Go home that night and write it all down, make a video, or get out your sketchbook. When we're in a state of chaos, when our emotions aren't in check, our inclination is to forget all the details that got us there. We just want out. But what separates good leaders from relational leaders is that they've developed the practices to lean in hard when the going gets tough and to learn from it.

PUT A FRESH LENS ON YOUR CHALLENGE

Now that we've identified the signs of organizational distress and dis-cussed some practices for navigating them, let's talk troubleshooting. A good relational leader is skilled at looking at problems in a variety of ways. They know that expanding the number of perspectives they use to look at a problem helps solve it. They don't just rely on their expe-rience; they find ways to continually recalibrate it by asking questions and incorporating fresh ways to appreciate what's going on around them.

The more lenses you apply to a problem, the faster you will gain clarity. The question is, What lenses are you using when faced with a thorny situation? Use this handy checklist below to make sure you are covering all the bases by using cognitive, social, political, and emo-tional lenses to ask good troubleshooting questions. Also, make sure to invite your team to weigh in with their own lenses so that they feel they are part of the solution.

- Using the cognitive lens, ask these questions:
  - What do **I know** about the problem?
  - What do **others know** about this problem?
  - How am **I evaluating** the problem?
  - How are **others evaluating** this problem?

- Using the social lens, ask these questions:
  - How do **I see** the problem?
  - How do **others see** the problem?
  - How is the problem **affecting relationships** on the team?
  - What **obstacles** are stopping us from moving ahead?
- Using the political lens, ask these questions:
  - What do **I see as the politics** of the problem?
  - What do **others see as the politics** of the problem?
  - What **judgments and assumptions have I** made about this problem?
  - What **judgments and assumptions have others** made?
- Using the emotional lens, ask these questions:
  - How do **I feel** about the problem?
  - How do **others feel** about the problem?
  - What **negative emotions** are around this problem?
  - How do I **channel positive energy** from this problem?

Most of us in North America tend to look at things through a *cognitive* lens that helps us identify missing information, fill in the blanks, and simplify problems by creating mental shortcuts.[65] It's critical for leaders to use their cognitive lens to call out and understand how the "givens" we bring into the workplace affect our judgment. This is where we form assumptions about the future, imagine alternative paths, and assess the consequences of those.[66] But a caution here: leaders who rely too much on this lens can find themselves overlooking the nut of the problem. These leaders become arbitrators of "fact wars," never fully appreciating what's really going on. This is why, in addition to the cognitive lens, we need to use these three others.

The *social* lens shapes impressions, attitudes, and codes of conduct and determines what is "right" and "wrong," "good" and "bad." It's deeply personal. And it's why two people in the same situation often see things differently. A myriad of factors contribute to these differences, including our background and experience, race, culture, religion, and economic status. At its best, the social lens helps us to

notice not just *differences* but also *similarities*. The social lens becomes the *connector* that brings people's hearts, minds, and intentions together.

The *political* lens focuses on the organization's power structures,
growing our understanding of how power influences people and situations. This lens encourages us to look at a problem in the context of
the entire ecosystem we are part of. The information we glean through
this lens helps us dissect our role in shaping outcomes and identify
sources of conflict and competing interests. As we gain insight into
patterns of power and how people exercise their power formally and
informally, we can better identify those who may be wielding undue
influence and control.

The *emotional* lens helps us identify, accept, manage, and communicate our emotions. In turn, this understanding helps us recognize
and appreciate others' emotional signals. We use our emotional lens
to regulate responses to situations that arise in the workplace. There
are three elements to pay attention to when using our emotional lens:
alerting, which relates to our ability to deal with emotions like anger
and fear; an *orienting response*, which helps when we undertake environmental scanning; and *executive attention*, which helps us select
and focus our attention on what we feel is most relevant.[67]

Relational leaders use their emotions to guide thoughts, actions,
and perspectives rather than as an excuse for impulsive reactions.
Research suggests that channeling emotions can alter how we attend
to things and influence the way we respond to the world around us.[68]
By tuning in to specific types of emotion, we become better at analyzing tricky situations. When we model this behaviour, it helps the team
to better manage themselves and their own relationships.

We also know that using the emotional lens can act as an early
warning system of growing stress and anxiety or even more serious
health conditions. In the age of well-being, we all need to become
better at using this lens to pick up on signals from our bodies. From
muscle tension and heart rate to feeling fear or pain, that's our emotional lens checking in to say, "Hey, go easy on yourself. Go easy on
others." Emotional reactions to negative stimuli reveal the fallout we
see in today's workplaces: everything from high blood pressure, heart
disease, and asthma to irritable bowel syndrome and ulcers. All can

be linked with the instantaneous responses we have to various high-stress situations.[69]

As empathy expert Cris Beam suggests, next time you have an emotional dustup with a coworker, one way to use your emotional lens is to repeat back to them exactly what they've said without editorializing or overdramatizing.[70] Listening to yourself say their words and then playing the tape back in your mind to hear the effects of your words is a humbling experience.

LEARNING HOW TO ESCAPE THE MESSY MAZE

No one wants to see their team fumble their way through a tricky project. It takes a leader who has a strong sense of the short-, medium-, and long-term journey and the guts to get there. Scott Belsky, Adobe's chief product officer, believes that when you embark on a challenging or new project, there are three phases to master: "enduring, optimizing and staring down the final mile."[71]

Staying the course is tough. It's easier to come up with excuses about why a shortcut here and there is the best way forward when the going gets tough. There are even some days when we feel we should quit altogether. You'll likely ask yourself a question that I've often posed myself: "Is this the hill to die on?"

But by now you know that these times are moments of truth. It's here you need to lay the facts out and make sense of them. Look long enough and you'll find the way out because you took the time to get to the root of the problem. That's your ticket out of the maze. Learning to play the long game isn't easy when everything needs to get done yesterday. It's here you'll need to develop effective communication with your boss and the team, walking them through the steps you are taking and absorbing their insights along the way. While you're making sense of the hot mess you're in, be sure to keep making decisions, even if they are microdecisions. Small moves and adjustments will keep the project moving forward while you figure out your next big moves. By facing moments of adversity, you'll find that you become your most resilient, creative, and innovative. Being able to pull the nose of the plane up will distinguish you as a leader who delivers.

Once you've committed to stay the course, focus on maximizing learning—for everyone. Remember when we talked about the idea that we are all leading all of the time? Well, when we're in the messy maze, *we all need to be learning all of the time.* I can't tell you how many mazes I got thrown into in my career where I was compelled to learn new "hard" and "soft" skills. Some organizations formalize these opportunities by providing "stretch assignments"; if you have a chance to take one on, you won't regret it. Because it's in these moments that you will grow. You'll realize where you're strong—and where you fall short. If learning opportunities are hard to come by in your organization, volunteer for a role in your community or join a committee in an association. As you rise in the ranks, be that leader who inspires learning for others.

Once you've committed to stay the course and maximize learning, the true test of leadership comes when you summon all your remaining energy to get the project over the line. Often during these moments, you can see the light at the end of the tunnel, but it still seems miles away. You're pooped but need to keep up the spirits of your equally exhausted team. These are "make or break" moments. This is when you'll be glad you developed practices to navigate complexity and troubleshoot. You've forged strong relationships with others, learned how to pause to gain distance, reflected on your learning, and drawn from multiple perspectives to inform your decisions. By mastering these practices, you'll have not only made better choices but also earned the trust of your team.

◆ ◆

Here's an example of a moment of truth where I had to learn how to use the four lenses to navigate and troubleshoot my way out of a tricky situation.

During my time with Retail Council of Canada (RCC), I had been asked to attend a press conference where one of our long-standing partners, the J.C. Williams Group, was presenting the findings of a national retail study. It was the first time such a study had been done in Canada, and the firm had invested a lot of time and resources to pull it off.

I'd received a call the day before from John Williams.* I can still hear his gravelly voice on the phone, asking, then pretty much insisting, that Retail Council appear at the presser to lend our voice to the study. He was a hard guy to say no to. I talked it over with Diane Brisebois, RCC's CEO, whom you met earlier, and we ended up with what we thought was a good compromise. I'd show up, but RCC wouldn't speak. I phoned John to explain our position, and he was clearly disappointed.

I made my way to the event and found myself in a swanky hotel ballroom. The hour was early, the lights were bright, and the room was packed with reporters and retailers. I took a seat close to the back of the room and watched John go through the high-level results.

Suddenly, he gestured to me at the back of the room and said, "And now, we'd like to invite Jill Birch from the Retail Council of Canada to join us here on stage to give her views on the results of the study." Every head turned to where I was seated. I stood and walked toward the podium that seemed a mile away. The room was silent. My mind was racing with a mix of emotions—*surprise* that he would ask me to speak knowing we'd discussed that I wouldn't, *fear* of messing up on such a public platform, and *anticipation* that I might actually be in a snippet of the evening news. That walk up to the podium was a *lonely* one, a moment of truth to be sure.

As I walked toward the stage, my cognitive lens whirred into motion, summoning the key facts and points John had just made. The social lens helped me completely recalibrate the situation I now found myself in. I was no longer an observer but a participant—whether I liked it or not. The political lens kicked in, and I remember deliberately *pausing*, but only for enough time to think that whatever I said better reflect well on my organization. The lights were so bright I couldn't see the audience—probably a good thing. And that's where the emotional lens saved me: I don't know how or why it happened, but there was a distinct moment when I said to myself that I needed to channel my nervous energy into a positive performance. I remember taking a

---

* John Williams was a pioneer in retail consulting and a dear colleague. John passed away while on a road trip with his brothers, Donald and Paul, on the last day of summer 2019. Near the end of their trip, the brothers stopped for ice cream, John's favourite food. John died peacefully in the car with his brothers at his side.

deep breath. And then . . . I simply launched. I spoke off the cuff for what was probably five minutes but felt like fifteen. I felt numb but oddly elated as John shook my hand and thanked me. I felt a swell of relief as the TV lights dimmed. With the press conference over, a new emotion—anger—grabbed me. Boy, that John would have some 'splaining to do.

John got what he wanted, and what did I get that day? Whether I liked it or not, a lesson in how to navigate by *acting in and on the moment.* We've all had these kinds of similar but different moments in our work lives—times when we think we are in control or even a couple of beats ahead of things. Suddenly out of nowhere, we find ourselves in sticky situations. When I look back at that moment, I see how those powerful experiences are not only leadership lessons but *life lessons.*

◆ ◆

Let's tap into an early story from Michael Hirsh, CEO of WOW!, who pioneered the development of thirty-minute cartoons around the world. You likely know his award-winning work for *Inspector Gadget* or the *Doodlebops.* Cartoons helped him see that *anything is possible,* a philosophy that has helped his team become fearless in overcoming big challenges.

> Michael: I think my leadership style was very influenced by cartoons even before I went into it. I thought of Bugs Bunny and the Road Runner, how they could do physically impossible things. There'd be a valley, but they could see the cliff on the other side. And as long as they didn't look down, they could walk across the chasm. I absorbed that. I tell young executives that story. When we're having a problem, I always tell them that story.
>
> Because the truth is, often to get to the other side of a problem, you can't look down and think the worst is going to happen. You have to see how you are going

to solve the problem. So, I've led in large part by using cartoons as examples to help inspire executives to accomplish what they think is possible. You have to be convinced you will come up with a solution, however bleak things might look.

Jill: And how do you do that?

Michael: I go into a deep think about what the problem is. And I think of all the permutations and solutions. And then I decide on a step one, step two, step three, and I try to break it down into steps. And then I organize people to execute. Sometimes it's a combination, sometimes it's just me, depending on the circumstance.

In Michael's story we see him building confidence within his team, appealing to them to think positively and imaginatively in order to envision possibility and see what's on the other side of their problem.

We also see Michael developing *step-by-step* plans, knowing when to include others in the process and when to tackle a problem on his own. Next time you're facing a thorny problem, urge yourself to look straight out ahead—don't look down!

CREATING YOUR SYSTEM TO NAVIGATE COMPLEXITY

Jake Gold, CEO of The Management Trust, shares this story about how he and his partner at the time, Allan Gregg, made decisions about rock bands who had *it* and those who didn't.

Jake: The greatest thing I've learned over the years is when not to get involved.

Jill: What helps determine that?

Jake: I remember when I worked with young bands, I would always send them down East for a month. Usually a week in a city. Some shitty little bars, three sets a night. And if they could handle it, if they came

back together as a band, then I knew, "OK, they passed
the test." These guys [a band he stopped managing]
failed the test. And they were blaming me for failing
the test. I said, "You guys don't get it."

I've seen this before and I know how it will play
out. If I back off it and let it play out, it ends up exactly
the way I want it to be without me getting involved.
That's my insight over the years. I say this to myself all
the time. If there's one thing I've learned, it's when to
walk away from something.

In Jake's story we see a leader who has learned to stare down the
final mile. First he developed a system based on his experience. We
get the feeling that he likely wasted time over the years on bands that
wouldn't make it. Once that happened a few times, he began to think
about ways to test them and determine their level of commitment. As
the tests evolved, he started seeing patterns emerge that were good
indicators of a band's potential. And Jake also had a trusted partner
he could bounce ideas off. With these pieces in place, Jake was able to
take in the full measure of a band.

PERFORMING VERSUS SLOWING DOWN

Ginny Dybenko was a top performer at a major telecommunications
company when she left to take on the leadership role of dean of the
business school at Wilfrid Laurier University. Ask anyone who has
made the leap from the private sector to a large complex public insti-
tution, and they'll tell you it's a whole new world. Should leaders jump
into action quickly and demonstrate their skills, or should they take
more time to get the lay of the land and understand the dynamics and
culture? Let's see what happened in Ginny's case:

I had the opportunity to head up the business school
at Wilfrid Laurier University. I was totally unprepared
for leadership in a university coming from an extended

corporate career. Looking back, I wouldn't have done anything for the first year. I would have just listened. After that year I would have started to think about vision and strategy with a full series of consultative roundtables. I'm always in a hurry.

I didn't have time to build a relationship with the president. I could see clearly what needed to be done and it ultimately resulted in great change. I had a clear mandate from the provost, who reported to the president. He gave me a lot of rope and I ran with it, but he wasn't too pleased with the results.

—*Ginny Dybenko, former dean, School of Business and Economics, Wilfrid Laurier University*

As we've seen, there are two sides to every story. In Ginny's story we see the classic conundrum that a new leader faces: the very real pressure to perform while simultaneously needing to slow down to get to know the organization. In this case we see how the political, social, emotional, and cognitive lenses collide, sending mixed messages that are often hard to decipher. The provost and president were urging her to forge ahead, but as quickly as Ginny made moves to change things, she was met with equal force to keep things the same. She became "othered." What would you have done if you were Ginny? Focusing on developing a strong internal network of supporters might have saved her from colleagues' intent to fight change. We also see in her reflections that taking the pulse of the organization and pausing would have helped her navigate the politics. With hindsight, Ginny acknowledged that in the first year she wouldn't have "done anything"—except listen. Even though she could clearly see what needed to be done, devoting time to developing relationships, hosting smaller intimate "get to know you" meetings, and facilitating more formal forums would have helped her socialize her ideas before getting into action. What Ginny's story tells us about navigating complexity is that it's important to slow down and take the pulse of the organization. It's also vital to take the time to understand and navigate the politics.

PRACTICE NAVIGATING COMPLEXITY

Here's my seven-step practice you can use to navigate complexity:

- **Step 1: Develop a long-term view.** Think through scenarios. Map out three or four possible outcomes and identify what plans will need to be in place for each scenario. Map out best and worst possible outcomes. Don't fall into the trap of assuming this new project will be the same as others. The context will be different, and new people will bring varying degrees of expertise and knowledge—and baggage.

- **Step 2: Before you start, look for team deficiencies.** Assess the strengths and weaknesses of the team and conduct training; build confidence and pride by holding forums to communicate the importance of the project and what it will mean to the organization; clearly lay out roles and responsibilities and decision-making rights.

- **Step 3: Become a dangerous expert.** Get to the bottom of problems fast by drilling down. This is not the time for a superficial assessment. Consider who you may need to bring in to provide more depth in specific areas where the team isn't as strong. Then develop the questions that will help you understand and mitigate risks.

- **Step 4: Keep your boss and peers informed.** Never surprise the boss. Hold regular check-in meetings to bring people up to date on how things are going. Be honest about obstacles and unanticipated problems. Deliver bad news early. Frame these obstacles as learning opportunities for all, remembering our discussion earlier about "failing forward."

- **Step 5: Help people "fail forward."** Lean heavily on the coaching skills you have developed. Let people know that

you understand mistakes are going to happen. Design
a rigorous and robust process to learn from mistakes.
Regularly check in to identify obstacles and bottlenecks
and clear the path for the team. That's your number one
job here.

- **Step 6: Prepare for "holy shit" moments.** If your project
  has fallen off a cliff, start with the four lenses. Determine
  the courses of action available, and lay out accompanying
  strategies that will help you execute. If you've decided to
  walk away, bulletproof your decision with sound rea-
  soning and extensive research, and call in experts for
  guidance and credibility. It's up to you to instill calm and
  confidence in the team. That can-do attitude needs to be
  carried through to the *next* project.

- **Step 7: Forgive yourself and others.** We all have experienced an epic fail. How we emerge from these challenges
  is the ultimate mark of leadership. Don't be bitter. Don't
  blame. Learn from what happened and share it with others. You'll be better off, and so will they.

Evaluate Your Performance

Here are a few key questions to ask yourself in order to successfully navigate the messy maze:

- Think about your behaviour in projects you have been involved in recently. What setbacks did you encounter?

  _____

  _____

  _____

- What was the root cause of the setbacks?

  _____

  _____

  _____

- What methods did you use to troubleshoot the problem?

  _____

  _____

  _____

- How did you reconnect, hear concerns, and reenergize the group?

- How did you set about making course corrections? Did they work?

- Based on your experience sizing up the situation, which of the four lenses do you need to develop more? How will you do that?

- As you consider the troubleshooting skills of enduring, optimizing, and staring down the final mile, where do you excel? Where do you need further development?

CHAPTER 7

Practice Becoming a Disruptive Innovator

> You can't connect the dots looking forward; you can only connect them looking backwards. So, you have to trust that the dots will somehow connect in your future.
>
> —*Steve Jobs, business magnate, inventor*

Steve Jobs, Elon Musk, and Sir Richard Branson became household names because they saw a future the rest of us couldn't quite grasp. They each had an uncanny knack for looking at the world differently. These disruptive innovators created products that people *didn't even know they needed*, underscoring the maxim that when you get it right, you not only become a first mover but can achieve rock star status. While you may not be aspiring to be like Jobs, Musk, or Branson, it's clear that the ability to innovate and to inspire innovation in others is a leadership capability in high demand. This chapter will provide you with behaviours, tools, questions, and practices that will help kick-start your innovation practice.

When I analyzed the work of disruptive innovators, they all seem to share five traits:

- They are enthusiastic problem hunters.
- They are obsessive about finding solutions.
- They never give up.
- They are not afraid to stand up for what they believe in.
- They are willing to make supreme sacrifices.

SOMETIMES INNOVATION IS A LIFE-AND-DEATH SITUATION

There were many stories of grit and tenacity that inspired us during the pandemic. One that caught my imagination was the story of two researchers who pioneered the discovery of the mRNA vaccine. Imagine the emotions flowing on December 18, 2021, when Dr. Kati Karikó and her fellow researcher Dr. Drew Weissman rolled up their sleeves to receive their COVID vaccinations; when the doctors and nurses of the hospital soon followed, Dr. Karikó wept. Countless lives were saved by Dr. Karikó and her fellow researchers, buoyed by their steadfast belief in each other and their resiliency to keep on going for over forty years.

Dr. Kati Karikó exemplifies disruptive innovation.[72] She could see what others could not. As I learned more about her arduous struggle, I saw in her the qualities of a relational leader who wouldn't quit. She didn't do it alone: she developed a small group of peers who supported each other through the years when many doubted their research. She had a positive, fail-forward attitude: her mentor Dr. David Langer commented, "The best scientists try to prove themselves wrong. Kate's genius was a willingness to accept failure and keep trying, and her ability to answer questions people were not smart enough to ask." Dr. Karikó sacrificed: she was so convinced that they were on to something that she was willing to accept incredibly low compensation for her work. She challenged the status quo: she said, "When your idea is against conventional wisdom that makes sense to the star chamber, it is very hard to break out." She lived for the lab: Dr. Karikó's passion came through in her mantra, "You are not going to work—you are going to have fun!"

A gifted Hungarian biochemist, she arrived in the US in her twenties fixated on mRNA cell research, a little-known field of study at the time. She was an enthusiastic problem hunter who found herself so obsessed with finding solutions that, forty years later, at the age of sixty-six, she finally received global recognition for her contributions to rolling out COVID vaccines.

Dr. Karikó faced a long and lonely road against incredible odds and largely without support. She was forced to move from lab to lab. Few bought into her unconventional ideas. But throughout it all, she was not afraid to *stand up* and *stand out* for what she believed in. And she never gave up.

If there was any good that came out of the pandemic, it was that we learned to innovate on the fly; the challenge now is to *sustain* those behaviours. It's not going to be easy. A McKinsey study showed that while new ideas are the key to growth, fewer than 30% of executives surveyed felt confident that they were prepared to address the changes they see coming.[73] One of the major reasons for this is that few leaders have actually developed a practice for rapid innovation. In today's competitive world, we know that consumers are making purchasing decisions based on how much they perceive an organization innovates.[74] It's not enough to be successful today; your organization's future success depends on sustaining and nurturing the mindset of a disruptive innovator.

DEVELOP A THEORY OF THE FUTURE

What's your theory on the future of your industry? According to late innovation pioneer Clayton Christensen, this is the first question we need to ask ourselves as we begin to innovate. In Clayton's view, once you've puzzled through this question and answered it the best you can, your practice should focus on mastering three critical elements:[75]

- Create enabling technology (an invention or innovation that makes a product or service more affordable and accessible to a wider population).
- Generate a dynamic business model (targeting new customer categories).
- Develop a cohesive value network (enrich your ecosystem so that suppliers, partners, distributors, and customers are *each better off* when the disruptive tech prospers).

It was this game-changing approach that helped Steve Jobs successfully disrupt the nascent cell phone market. Jobs's view of the future of his industry was that a phone should fit easily in your pocket and in your hand. He identified the bulky, inelegant design of those early phones as his major problem. Initially, he created a mash-up between an iPod and a cell phone. It didn't work.

Unhappy with its look and feel, he one day randomly came upon a group of Apple engineers trying to help people with physical disabilities. They were working on a breakthrough technology called "iGesture" (a way to use your fingers to launch applications). It was a eureka moment for Jobs. He combined the iPod and cell phone design with iGesture innovation, and the iPhone was born.

But there was still something holding Jobs back. He didn't want to partner with other organizations to develop apps. Eventually, he overcame his hesitancy to allow third parties to develop apps, building a value network that's now pegged at $643 billion.[76] This is a story that shows the importance of connecting the dots, harnessing technology, empowering dedicated teams of people to innovate, and enriching your ecosystem. But it's also a story of the importance of not trying to control everything. If Jobs hadn't opened up apps to outside developers, Apple would never have realized its level of market domination.

Today's innovators will become the leaders of tomorrow. Why? Because they see a future that helps their company provide unique and better products and services for their customers. Whether you come up with the idea or you are leading a team to bring these break-throughs to life, the act of launching the innovation will distinguish you from others.

In addition to the five traits we covered at the start of this chapter, successful leaders need to develop behaviours to support their teams in the innovation process. The first step is to understand the obstacles that can and do derail successful innovation. It's all well and good to be open to new ideas, but it's imperative to create a framework that en-sures accountability, an honest and constructive feedback system, and a structured decision-making process. Read on to learn how to create a thriving, healthy, productive innovative process.

Begin by defining innovation, both inside your industry and outside of it. Start creating digital files or make collages of exam-ples that reflect the kind of big thinking and quantum leaps that your organization could learn from. Next, become a student of in-novation by assessing your own level of understanding of how in-novation works. Visit organizations like IDEO and the Institute for the Future; study their design thinking processes. Start by keeping up with the latest trends in innovation. Follow what's happening in innovative technology like artificial intelligence, the Internet of Things, and Blockchain. Bookmark designers, artists, and thinkers that you find impressive.

Now ask yourself about your prowess as an innovator. What inno-vation are you most proud of? What was the spark that got it all going? What steps did you take to bring it to life? Who and what influenced you? Ask these questions and they will help you develop the disrup-tor's stance.

Think about the kinds of innovation that would really make a dif-ference in your organization. Should you focus on a product or service innovation? If you're lagging behind the competition, maybe you need a daring marketing campaign or an unconventional business model or radical process innovation.

Once you've decided on the kind of innovation you want to ex-plore, have candid conversations with your team about the upsides and downsides of innovation processes. Innovating is fun as teams are encouraged to step outside comfort zones and colour outside the lines, but teams also need to take responsibility for outcomes. Be clear on your metrics. Hold regular project assessment reviews to build both alignment and accountability.

Compromise and analysis paralysis have condemned many an innovation project to the waste bin. Leaders need to help teams wade through the murkiness of "consensus" and "collaboration." Set up a charter for decision-making before your innovation project gets underway. Decide ahead of time who the ultimate decision-maker is, who needs to give consent, and who should be informed. Be on the lookout when teams start blaming each other or progress is stalled because people can't agree on a direction. Lastly, take full responsibility. Pledge to innovation projects for the long term. This means developing new stores of patience, monitoring progress, and looking for opportunities for training and development. As a leader, you bear the ultimate responsibility when things go wrong; take a page out of the J&J credo: "You take the risk, I take the blame."

Now let's look at three stories where we see disruptive leadership traits supported by the disciplined behaviour required to successfully innovate.

FIND YOUR MOMENT OF CLARITY

Sometimes a chance encounter can lead to innovation. What we see in this next story, though, is that it takes a lot more than randomly meeting up with people to create a disruptive innovation. Relying on our experience and drawing on insights from conversations are vital to connecting the dots to help you see into the future. Oh, and a bit of luck never hurts. That moment came for Paul Alofs during a once-in-a-lifetime meeting with Steve Jobs and John Lasseter.* At the time, Paul

---

* John Lasseter began his career at Walt Disney but was fired for promoting computer animation. He joined Lucasfilm, where he worked on groundbreaking CGI animation, which was then sold to Steve Jobs and became Pixar. The films he made have grossed more than $19 billion, making him one of the most successful filmmakers of all time. Now that's a story of gaining distance and meeting resistance.

was running all the Disney stores in North America. It was 1999 and a guy named Shawn Fanning had just launched a little project called Napster.

> There was like six or seven of us sitting in a small boardroom. And it was one of those moments in time. And I just thought, you know, who in hell would compete in animation with the Walt Disney company? Lasseter actually got pushed out [of Disney] because of his beliefs in using technology in animation. But then I also thought, who would invest $20 million to back this guy to go into competition? Well, that would be Steve Jobs. He was going back to Apple, even after he was pushed out.
>
> So, in that moment in time I saw what it was all about . . . being able to organize and focus your passion. And I also saw you need to do it with clarity.
>
> —*Paul Alofs, retired CEO,*
> *Princess Margaret Hospital Foundation*

The moment of clarity occurred as Paul focused on his passion: music. That encounter fused Paul's experience with his passion for song, nudging him to explore the impact of tech advances on the music industry. You see, before Disney, Paul was the CEO of HMV Music and BMG Music Canada. These positions afforded him a ringside seat to the big shifts that occurred as people moved from vinyl records to CDs. Digital downloads were in their infancy, but Paul reasoned that if the world of animation was changing, then there would likely be big changes in how music would be distributed.

The next disruptive clue came serendipitously. While still working at Disney, he ran into a colleague in the parking lot after work and stopped to say hi. That parking lot chat led to his epiphany that the music industry's business model was about to implode; with that insight, Paul became part of the management team that founded MP3. com, which launched for $400 million in 1999,[77] one of the most successful internet IPOs ever. Paul's early recognition that the internet was going to change everything set him on a path to become one of Canada's leading disruptive innovators.

Success like Paul's won't happen for all of us. It's important to remember that not all epiphanies will take flight. But if you *pause* to take in the moment, *plan* out scenarios of how things might take shape, and *prepare* to take calculated risks, you just might have a winner on your hands.

PROVOKE DISRUPTION BY PLAYING AROUND

Artist Alex McLeod shared an innovation story that began one night when he found himself playing around with different ideas on his computer.

> Recently on Instagram I've been including this little character, which is outside what I normally do. And instantly I encountered huge opposition, but then, also huge support, like "Oh my God, I'm really into this!" The character caused a reaction.
>
> It was an opening that I wasn't looking for. There's this technology that caused this riff. And I thought, "OK, I'm going to keep poking at it." And then I was called by a senior vice president to do a campaign. I've got a gallery in New York who's asking for it and it's all happening because of that little pocket. It's so exciting. This would have never been possible before.
>
> —*Alex McLeod, artist*

Up until this moment, Alex's art was devoted to creating flourishing digital landscapes that conveyed a sense of joy. As he says, "Landscape art comes from being present in your environment, not knowing what's next and just appreciating the natural change of everything—that's how I interpret it."[78] Alex is right—as leaders, we don't know what is going to happen next or how things will evolve. We can't predict the influences that will change how we—or our custom-ers—will respond to things. But what we can do is hone our abilities to observe, listen, and appreciate what's going on around us. We can make adjustments. Change how we approach things. See that we're in a rut and get out of it. To do that, though, we need to shake ourselves up.

We need to create *a moment of provocation* for ourselves. We can't ask others to innovate unless we're the first to demonstrate that it's OK to escape our comfort zone.

Alex's moment arrived simply because he had decided to "play around." Alex's innovation developed as an outgrowth and extension of his regular practice; he gained distance from regular routines in de-veloping art and started experimenting with new ways to use tech-nology. Alex *disrupted himself.* Who knows, he might have even been bored and just wanted to do something different for a change. In giv-ing himself latitude to move out of his usual artistic process, he fell into a new innovation process and created a little animated character that caused reactions he wasn't prepared for.

And Alex had a choice; he could have listened to the opposition of his followers and quit or been cheered on by those who were into it. He took a calculated risk to keep going, which then led to commissions with companies like Nike, Samsung, and Condé Nast. Not bad for just playing around with a "little character."

In our final innovation example, I will share the story of how Shauna Levy, former CEO of the Design Exchange, developed EDIT, which stands for Exhibition for Design, Innovation, and Technology. In 2012, when Shauna started her new role, she was handed a strate-gic plan that included a major initiative to launch a design festival in Toronto. She began by asking the innovator's question: "What does the future of design look like?" As she scanned the horizon, she had two aha moments. The first was that accessibility was an issue: peo-ple are often intimidated to visit design houses and museums. They worry they "won't get it" and as a result may feel embarrassed. Shauna set out to disrupt this tendency by creating an experience that people could relate to. She wanted to showcase the best examples of design having a positive impact on the world by making this exhibition as engaging as it was entertaining. Her second observation was that the worlds of design, innovation, and technology were converging. What better way to demonstrate innovation than by inviting designers from around the world to show off their ingenuity in these three merging areas?

And with that, EDIT was born—a ten-day festival focusing on solutions to global problems addressed by design innovations.

These two insights arrived right when Shauna was researching the United Nations' 17 Sustainable Development Goals, which prompted a third insight. Shauna realized that her innovation would require massive support: "It became clear to me that we were only going to be able to do this if government, corporations, and people came together." That conclusion led to a meeting with officials at the United Nations, where she presented the EDIT concept in such a way that it would address the UN goals through design. The UN came on board as a partner, giving Shauna instant credibility to approach others.

That next opportunity to create an innovative partnership arose when Shauna posed a gutsy question in a very public forum on International Women's Day. She asked Katie Telford, chief of staff to the prime minister of Canada, what the federal government was doing to meet the United Nations' goals, particularly in the context of gender parity. That question led to a new round of funding to make EDIT a reality. With partnerships struck and funding in place, Shauna then assembled and led a team that built an event that attracted thousands of visitors in the fall of 2017. Never one to pass up an opportunity for further innovation, Shauna closed out the exhibition with "Feeding the 5,000"—a feast menu that gathered all the food on site that otherwise would have been wasted and put it to good purpose in the community. Now that's full-circle innovation.

THE HAMSTER WHEEL WILL NEVER LEAD TO INNOVATION

Most of us are on a hamster wheel in a typical workday. Day in, day out, we're in meetings, we work the phones, check email, and toil away on initiatives to reach targets and goals. Making the time to create an "off ramp" from the regular routine of your "busy" day is crucial to developing a nose for innovation.

Detaching yourself from routine like Alex McLeod did is a

powerful way to innovate. These are the moments when we're able to play with ideas and wonder more deeply about possibilities. Try being more deliberate in your approach to innovation and take the "blink test." I've used this technique in my own work and with countless clients. It's a simple and effective way to innovate. I call it the blink test because it's a way to put distance between yourself and an immediate problem you may be dealing with. Often we fixate on the issue in front of us, not giving ourselves the breathing room required to reframe what the problem really is. Remember earlier in the book when we talked about the power of pausing, planning, and preparing? This is another way you can use the 3 Ps to help you become more innovative by imagining not what is but *what could be.*

The first step is to find a spot where you are away from distractions. If there's an abandoned meeting room on the tenth floor, claim it. Lock yourself in. You don't have to do this alone. If you have a team of colleagues who can help you with a problem, bring them with you.

Let's use the example of improving a new hire's onboarding experience. The "blink test" begins by clearing your mind, closing your eyes, and letting yourself drift. Some people go on excursions, taking a ton of pictures that they feel reveal the heart of the problem. The important point here is to give yourself that time to pause and detach from the stress and pressure of trying to find an immediate "answer." Rather, pretend that this is the first time you are encountering the problem. So, *forget your existing onboarding process—it doesn't exist.* Forget the internet's "top ten onboarding tips."

Think about the total experience of a new employee walking through your doors on the first day of their new job. Think about what led up to that moment. They've gone through quite a vetting process. They are likely a combination of nerves and excitement. How do you help them relax and take it all in? You may want to give that new employee a name and start to *build a persona.* Think about how they feel—and think about what they need to know to start off on the right foot. Dream about what you think would be the best onboarding experience in the world—ever!

Get into *planning* mode. *Write down every question* you think a new employee might have. Use your experience here—think about the questions you would ask, think of your own onboarding experiences.

Think also about the "firsts." Who should they meet first? What should they learn first? Respond to all the questions you've come up with in as much rich detail as you can. Bring stacks of Post-it notes and write down one idea per note. Throw those up on the wall. Move them around, mapping out what that first day could look like. Then take pictures of what you've created and begin to shop it around to gain others' reactions and ideas.

Now let's think about *preparing*. There's a caution on our well-conceived plan: while you will no doubt come up with solutions, you also need to think about how to *socialize your ideas* to gain acceptance. Your ideas might meet resistance, and you will need to prepare for that. This is where relational leadership can help you. Remember when we talked about the power of seeing through the eyes of others? This is a moment where you want to put on your compassion hat. Ask yourself what questions or objections your boss might have about what you're proposing. What about the human resources department? You would want to include them early in the process, engaging them as a thinking partner and stakeholder. Think about the people you work with and where they're coming from. Will your innovation be perceived as creating "more work" for them? Do your homework and have answers at the ready.

This is also the time to *test your resolve*: How much do you believe in your idea? How far will you go? Your innovation, no matter how big or small, might break rules; people might believe it will cause them more work; some may feel ownership over a product or service that they had a hand in creating. They don't want you messing with it! You may find yourself in a power struggle between departments. You may even find that you are fighting yourself, not just questioning whether it's all worth it but whether the idea is even good enough. Dr. Karikó's story is a good example of an innovator who stuck to her beliefs despite meeting resistance head-on. My observation is that when you feel that tension of butting up against existing ways of doing things or when you feel that resistance, you'll know you're on your way to innovating.

DEVELOP AN INNOVATION PROCESS

As we've seen, innovation begins when we envision a different future and we follow up with questions like "Why do things have to be this way?" and "What would happen if we tried a different approach?" and "What's a better way of doing this?" and "What's an easier way of doing this?" Innovation is also accompanied by processes. There are as many processes out there as there are innovation consultants. One process I like to work with was designed by Bill O'Connor, founder of the Genome Project at Autodesk.[79] Bill works with the LUMIAMI innovation process, which poses seven questions that will help you spark innovation conversations with your team:

- What could we **look** at in a new way to form a new perspective?
- What could we **use** in a new way?
- What could we **move**, changing its position in time and space?
- What could we **interconnect** in a different way or for the first time?
- What could we **alter** or change in terms of design and performance?
- What could we **make**, creating something that is truly new?
- What could we **imagine** to create a great experience for someone?

LET YOURSELF PLAY IN THE SANDBOX

There's a saying in Buddhism about approaching life with a "beginner's mind." The maxim "In the beginner's mind there are endless possibilities, but in the expert's mind there are few"[80] goes a long way to showing us how powerful *starting* can be when we think about how to innovate.

When a child is playing, they are taking material from their inner reality—or dreamworld—and placing it into external reality—or what we might call the *real world*. If we extend this to the workplace, the teams that play at the intersection of dream and reality are the ones who will more quickly identify opportunities for disruption.

A few summers back at our family cottage, I had an opportunity to see the beginner's mind in action. Our three-year-old twin grand-kids, Isla and Nora, discovered the shoe rack. The first thing they did, of course, was empty out all the shoes, about twenty-five pairs. The second thing they did was to start trying on all those shoes—size 10 flip-flops, size 7 Birkenstocks, and size 9 work boots. Then they found my size 5 sandals from Italy; the shoes were covered with colourful leather flowers of red, yellow, orange, and green. They hobbled around the kitchen, delighted to have found a pair that "worked," and with big bright flowers to boot. Their big smiles of happiness, the joy of discovery, and the newfound confidence of making a good choice had produced their own little eureka moment.

This silly little shoe story represents a way to discover, explore, and teach ourselves all at once. When you think about how you approach problems at work, give yourself permission not just to start over but to be that child again. Be that *natural starter*. Experiment, play make-believe, act out real-life situations, and colour outside the lines. Not only are these approaches a heck of a lot more fun, but they also offer ways to imaginatively see situations more as opportunities than problems.

Ask yourself what's missing. That's where kids are great—they fill gaps as fast as they encounter them. Iterative work helps you get as close as possible to your best and most informed guess at what may occur. According to Nicholas Negroponte, the most successful visits to his lab at MIT occur when corporate clients bring their kids. Lamenting that he could do executive "dog and pony" shows until the cows come home, Negroponte said it's when the kids are there that a new world opens up: "They [the clients] see things that are meaningful to their kid but not to them. So they pay more attention. I found that it was wonderful. I love it when people come with their kids."[81]

Developing a child's curiosity means asking questions like the following:

- What is this? I've never seen it before.

- What assumptions are we bringing to this problem?
- What's changed since we last encountered this problem?
- Why isn't it working the way we thought it would?
- What have we learned so far?
- Who's done something similar to this?
- How did they test it then?
- How do we test it now?

Ask more questions than you have answers for before you attempt to lock in on specific solutions. Generate as many ideas as you can, then helicopter up to look for themes and patterns. These insights will supply a rich assortment of approaches that will help you land on the ones that make the most sense.

PROXIMITY LEADS TO INNOVATION

Apple's learning campus was designed so that twelve thousand people could "connect and collaborate and walk and talk." This was purposeful. Apple's chief designer, Jonathan Ive, hoped that people would bump into one another and that this might lead to a great innovation.[82]

Many organizations seek more spontaneity with the hope that it will generate innovation but fail to lay the groundwork for it. Corporate offices aren't laid out in ways that create space for creativity. Teams aren't encouraged to cross-pollinate ideas and learn about what their colleagues are working on. Encouraging spontaneous insights means providing teams with places to meet up and proper time to play.

Still holding your meetings in windowless rooms with stiff plastic chairs and bad coffee? Don't expect too much. While not all organizations are as flush as Apple, small changes to your physical space can make a big difference.

Create room to move around. If you have a lot of cubicles, consider taking some down to open up space. This frees teams to run into each other and explore in ways that are random and unfiltered. Shake things up: take a deliberate break from stiff agendas that stifle, and instead create some open time to *drift*. Embolden teams to name and face fears as they embrace disruptive way to innovate. The benefits of working in this way are many: you'll save time thinking through things together; come up with different approaches; and most importantly, you won't feel the burden of having to come up with things all on your own. Having a team to collaborate with is not only energizing but is a great way to create breakthroughs.

Give people permission to daydream. Cancel that regular Monday-morning huddle you've held for the past five years. Clear the agenda of that standing marketing meeting that's held once a month. Get outside and leave the office behind. Take a field trip to an art gallery, arrange to meet artists, or visit a university's creative destruction lab. Expose your team to new and different sites, sounds, people, and viewpoints—all these situations spur creativity. If you can't get out, bring guest speakers in, hold contentious debates. Try things that deliberately shake people up, create new stimuli, and launch people out of their comfort zone.

VISUALIZATION: NOT JUST THE DOMAIN OF CREATIVE PEOPLE

I remember that one of my first meetings at OCAD University, Canada's largest art and design university, was with Archie Graham, the then head of the faculty union and now professor emeritus. I asked, "Archie, why would a donor give to OCAD U over another university?" Without missing a beat, he said, "Because other schools teach analytical thinking; here, we teach visual thinking." He had me at "visual."

My experiences at OCAD U and then later at the Canadian Art Foundation were instructive in helping me ask the most important question a disruptive innovator can ask: "What could be?" Little did I know when I started drawing, making collages, and taking photographs of how leadership might be understood that it would dramatically change not just my perspective but also how I learned. Visualization helped me identify opportunities I'd never seen before.

I know what you're thinking—*I'm no artist*. Well, neither am I. But according to designer Bruce Mau, it's a mistake to think of visualization as the domain of creative people. I had experienced both dead ends of the innovation process—"blank-screen-itis" and crawling through a deluge of data. And even if I was skeptical, I knew I had to try a new approach.

I was tentative about visualization at the beginning, but desperation eventually helped me lose my inhibitions. I can honestly say that drawing helped me see the relational practices I've laid out in this book. And it was this work that led me to what I now see as the most crucial part of the innovation process: crystallization. When things fall into place, it makes all the effort, struggle, and agonizing worth it.

Showing myself what the literature and my research were saying, what my advisors were proffering, and what I was thinking helped me *see* leadership in new ways. These simple acts of creation, regardless of their crudeness, positioned me to better leverage the innovation opportunities in front of me. You can do this too. Keep an unlined book with you at all times (I happen to prefer a moleskin) and have a batch of sticky notes and colourful pens on hand. Of course, you can also use a Wacom tablet and the Post-it app. Use whatever you're comfortable with. When you have an innovation challenge or get stuck on a problem, drawing is a great way to pause, giving you that much-needed distance between yourself and your challenge.

Here's an example of how visualization helped me get unstuck. I was trying to figure out how to help leaders use their stories to reveal relational leadership practices. Out of nowhere the image of an hourglass popped into my mind. I became intrigued by its properties as a container that could turn, flip, and pour the stories over and over again. There is no bottom or top to an hourglass. As it continually turns and pours sand from one end to the other, its contents (and our stories) are always shifting and *changing*. That helped me form a key insight: that when relational leaders become more comfortable in the *messy middle* of the hourglass, they are better able to innovate because they are able to see things from many angles. It was this insight that inspired the earlier chapter on navigating the messy maze. The hourglass, both the drawing and the metaphor, helped create the framework, practices, and "how-tos" in this book.

Bricolage is another technique that can help you visualize ideas in new ways. As I was interviewing leaders for this book, I created bricolages to show myself what I thought I was hearing. The French term *bricolage* roughly translates to "do it yourself" and refers to creating

ANALYSIS: A WAY TO SEE INSIDE

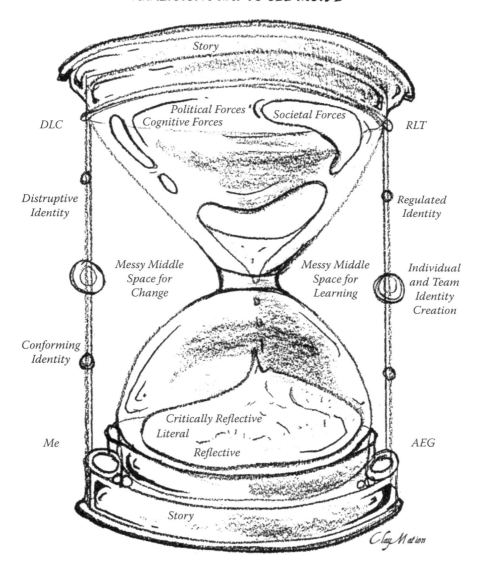

Using an hourglass as a way to visualize relational leadership

something from materials at hand. With over 1,600 pages of transcripts from the interviews I held with leaders, I occasionally felt overwhelmed. Getting to the nut of what these leaders were trying to tell me shaped the framework for the seven practices. But it took some time to get there. I ended up using bricolage to draw and redraw what I thought they were telling me. It was a way for me to become a more surgical listener, processing the images, stories, and emotions they shared.

PRACTICE BECOMING A DISRUPTIVE INNOVATOR

Here's a seven-step practice you can use to become a disruptive innovator:

- **Step 1: Audit your current innovation practice.** Learn and experiment with disruptive innovation practices like the LUMIAMI process. Assess how well you are currently balancing the five unique behaviours of innovation leadership. Be an enthusiastic problem hunter. Be obsessive about finding solutions; don't run from them! Never give up. Don't be afraid to stand up for what you believe. Be prepared to make supreme sacrifices.

- **Step 2: Be a problem hunter.** Make a list of the key challenges in your department and/or organization. Review the key innovations your organization has developed. Ask how they came to be and what people learned. Also make note of experiments that didn't go so well and analyze why that happened. Look for similar opportunities where you can replicate these processes. Gather local input and data that can act as a springboard to form your next innovation sprint.

- **Step 3: Be a problem solver.** Focus on developing a shared process with your team. When a common method is established, it gives people permission to brainstorm about ideas because they all agree on what they're fighting for; it also keeps things from becoming personal. Develop feedback loops that encourage innovation, and constantly iterate.

- **Step 4: Think like a beginner.** Don't dwell on past experiences. But do learn from them. As we look back, we may embellish what's happened or edit things out. Don't immediately accept assumptions; turn them over and examine them closely so that you don't jump to conclusions. Hang around with kids. Watch how they take in the world, and ask the kinds of questions they do: "Why is something a certain way?" "How does this work?"

- **Step 5: Develop rules of engagement.** Determine roles, responsibilities, and meeting and communication protocols ahead of the project launch. Clarify decision rights (who is responsible for executing, who is accountable for making decisions, who will be consulted, who will be informed). Map out project timelines, milestones, key decision points. Harness apps to ensure all voices are heard and there is a sense of collective accountability.

- **Step 6: Get outside.** Take people out to an art gallery, bring in actors to role-play, have people take photos or make things like collages that help them have fun while they're processing. Book a recording studio with a couple of songwriters, and have the team write songs with them. Experiences that take people out of the status quo make learning stick.

- **Step 7: Solicit feedback and constantly refine.** Every innovation effort is a learning opportunity. Disruptive leaders constantly infuse learning into team meetings, create great stories of what went right and wrong, and share their learning across the organization.

Evaluate Your Performance

As you begin your next innovation quest, ask yourself these key questions to build stronger practices:

- How are you developing your practice as a problem hunter?

  _____

  _____

  _____

- How are you keeping up with disruptive forces?

  _____

  _____

  _____

- Where do you turn to source out innovative solutions?

  _____

  _____

  _____

- Which of the disruptive skills do you want to further develop?

- Which disruptive innovative skills do you believe your team needs to learn more about?

- What does disruption look like in your industry?

- When you think about a time you were innovative, what happened to get you there?

- How are you gathering multiple perspectives to fuel innovation insights?

  _____

  _____

  _____

- How are you supporting the team to think like beginners?

  _____

  _____

  _____

- How is your current innovation process working, or do you need to develop one?

  _____

  _____

  _____

- When you think about a product or service at work that is not up to scratch, what would be a way to improve it?

  _____

  _____

  _____

- What processes are you currently using to develop, monitor, and measure innovation?

_____

_____

_____

CHAPTER 8

Practice Becoming a Selfless Leader

> There is an infinite number of possible futures. Which one will actually become the future? It's going to depend on how we behave now.
> —*Margaret Atwood, author*

CULTIVATE YOUR LEADERSHIP GARDEN

Twenty-first-century leaders can't be one-trick ponies. They need to amass a broad and expansive range of skills, knowledge, and experience that sets them and their organizations apart from others. There's no room for a leader who is only good at relationships or who only has a good head for strategy or numbers.

Today's leaders must have a deep understanding of how to alter their behaviour and refine their practices to meet each moment as it comes. This means being relentless in your dedication to develop yourself. It means being open to feedback—even when it might sting. It means that even though you may have been leading for a while, you never assume you know it all or have seen it all. You haven't. In fact, as we've seen, the longer we are leaders, the more comfortable and complacent we become. This is where the final practice of becoming a selfless leader helps to keep us sharp. This practice is a constant reminder that when we integrate all the relational behaviours, we become genuine difference makers.

Nelson Mandela was one of those relational leaders who was a master in each practice, and he left an indelible mark on the world. What sets him apart is that he spent his life *integrating* leadership behaviours in such a way that he saw possibility everywhere. Mandela spent twenty-seven years behind bars, eighteen of which were at Robben Island's Pollsmoor Prison off the coast of Cape Town, South Africa. Upon arrival, he found himself surveying a hot, neglected space on the building's roof, which was in sunlight every day. He had an epiphany that day and received permission from the commanding officer to start a garden.

As Mandela tells it: "In some ways, I saw the garden as a metaphor for certain aspects of my life. A leader must also tend his garden; he, too, plants seeds, and then watches, cultivates, and harvests the results. Like the gardener, a leader must take responsibility for what he cultivates; he must mind his work, try to repel enemies, preserve what can be preserved, and eliminate what cannot succeed."[83]

Each morning, Mandela would put on a straw hat and rough gloves and work in the garden for two hours. Every Sunday, he supplied vegetables to the kitchen so that they could cook a special meal for the common-law prisoners. Soon more prisoners joined to help, and eventually they had over nine hundred plants on the roof, which helped to feed the prisoners and their jailers.

Throughout those torturous years, Mandela decided to use the gifts of his leadership in a very positive way. Many leaders might give up, become pessimistic, and be depressed. Every day, each of us in our own way makes a choice about whether we will see things in a positive or negative light. It's this fundamental choice—of how we see the world and how we behave in it—that ultimately directs how well we support others and how we continue to grow in our career and as human beings. Mandela used his garden as a way to connect, be an example, create community, and make people feel less isolated.

Relational leaders must find ways to continually draw strength for themselves in order to encourage and inspire others. Mandela built up his resilience and commitment to his vision while in prison. And this gave him the strength to face the many obstacles he would encounter. Harvard Kennedy School's founding director, Robert Rotberg, described a crucial moment when rioters were preparing to act violently. Mandela was able to prevent race riots by telling them: "Listen to me, I am your leader, and I am going to give you leadership . . . As long as I am your leader, I will tell you, always, when you are wrong."[84]

It takes extraordinary skills to create a vision, forge connections between people, identify common goals, and rally people around those goals to take purposeful action. As you grow in your career, you will find that you will be asked to make greater sacrifices; more time will be needed to serve and help others. It's no longer about you; it's about supporting a greater goal. It's in making this leap from self-fulness to selflessness that you become an integrated relational leader.

Ukrainian president Volodymyr Zelensky is another example of an integrated relational leader. With bombs falling and casualties in both civilian and soldier populations, Zelensky taught the world a lesson on noble purpose. When the United States offered to airlift him out, he responded, "The fight is here; I need ammunition, not a ride."[85] With those words, Zelensky earned the trust of Ukrainians—and people around the world.

While most leaders will never face anything even close to what Volodymyr Zelensky is dealing with, there are still valuable lessons we can take away. He never gives himself a pass—not even on his hardest day. According to *Time* magazine reporter Simon Shuster, who spent two weeks with him in the spring of 2022, he is hardest on himself.[86] Each night as he retires to a cot in his bunker, he reviews his day's agenda and wonders whether he missed something or forgot to reach out to someone. He constantly reevaluates his priorities and where he needs to put his best efforts.

And he's always reflexive, asking himself what else he could have or should have done. Many leaders focus on the next day's agenda, but developing a disciplined review of the current day means that tomorrow's work will be more focused and purposeful. He makes it a point to get out and have people see him confronting the ravages of war. His courage gives others courage.

We could all take lessons from Zelensky's methods of communicating. From his first virtual address to the United Nations to a surprise virtual visit to the Oscars, his skillful performances are as authentic as they are galvanizing. We learn from him over and over again the importance of developing and delivering a consistent, well-articulated message. We see how he balances communications between external and internal audiences. We note how unshakingly positive he is, encouraging these audiences to be united in their resolve to keep going.

He uses social media extraordinarily well; at the beginning of the war, he used a simple video phone message to tell the world, "We are here . . . Defending our independence, our country."[87] Messages like this were defining moments of his early leadership, instantly cementing his credibility.

Of utmost importance, Zelensky proudly wears the burden of leadership. He knows the world is watching, commenting, "You understand that they're [the world is] watching. You're a symbol. You need to act the way a head of state must act."[88] It's interesting to note how he plays the part in his clothing, wearing sweaters and T-shirts, always in army green, and very much portraying himself as a wartime president. Another attribute is Zelensky's use of humour, which he uses intentionally to ease the endless tension around him.

How ironic that his TV show *Servant of the People* might have been so instrumental in helping him to become the servant leader that he is. The jury is out on what will happen in Ukraine. Can Zelensky maintain his energy? Will his message continue to resonate? This war that is now over a year old at the time of this writing will remain a rich field of study in leadership.

As we've seen in this example, the seventh practice is the hardest one. It's here that leaders work to integrate the six relational practices, strengthening themselves to "be" a leader rather than just looking or acting like one.

THE ULTIMATE COST OF FAILURE

A recent *MIT Sloan Management Review* article found that 50% of leaders will fail, paying the price for neglecting to grow themselves.[89] Researchers have also uncovered that the further you progress in your career, the less leadership development you will receive. To be a better leader, then, it's up to us to be constantly learning, growing ourselves and those around us. It is in the coaching of others that we strengthen our relational capabilities and keep ourselves plugged into what's happening out there. We also have to be on the lookout for the derailers we identified earlier that affect our performance and how we show up. We need to become architects of our own leadership, drawing up blueprints that document where we are and what we need to do to develop ourselves. It's up to us to become master integrators.

Even the greatest leaders are far from perfect. We've seen how vital it is to first build up our self-awareness, acknowledging where we've faltered, and then to do something about it. And that means changing our attitudes and our behaviours. It also means being real with yourself about how you absorb feedback and what you do with that feedback. The growing responsibility that goes along with promotions means you can never stop learning or changing. This is what it means to be an integrated relational leader.

Some would say that Elon Musk has what it takes to become a master integrator. Others disagree. Regardless of our personal feelings, there is no doubt Elon is a "many-trick pony." This is the person who almost single-handedly championed electric cars and built up a company worth more than Toyota, Honda, Volkswagen, Mercedes, BMW, Ford, and General Motors combined. But now storm clouds surround his company.

As I studied his behaviour in the closing months of writing this book, there was a lot going on in his life. New twins, the purchase of Twitter, and a growing number of lawsuits from people who had been killed by driverless Teslas.[90] I reviewed positive and negative comments about his leadership. And you know what? They all rang true.

That's why it's so vital for leaders to develop what I have come to call a healthy relational state. Self-awareness and compassion. Empowerment and nurturing culture. Navigating complexity and nurturing innovation. Fire on all these cylinders and you will have a better chance to achieve the ultimate goal of full integration.

There is no doubt Elon has made the world a better place. Think about the ties he has developed with Zelensky and Ukraine. His company Starlink possesses roughly half of the 3,335 active satellites in the world[91] and continues to support Ukraine's communications during the war. At an estimated cost of $400 million over a twelve-month period, that's a sizeable commitment. At one point he threatened to stop supporting Ukraine because of the cost but then said, "To hell with it . . . even though Starlink is still losing money . . . we'll just keep funding [the] Ukraine govt for free."[92] It's important to note here that Starlink is not carrying all the costs on its own; many other countries and companies are helping out. Elon admitted that and thanked them. This is the positive side we see in Elon. We see here, in full bloom, the practices of compassion, innovation, and navigating complexity.

But there's this other side of Elon we have come to know. He is a master at driving attention to all that he does. He's unabashed in his appraisal of himself. When a lawyer asked him in a recent deposition "Do you have some kind of unique ability to identify narcissistic sociopaths?" he replied, "You mean by looking in the mirror?"[93] When he assumed the role of chief twit at Twitter, the world had a front-row seat—through his Tweets—to follow his every action. He gave the "first ninety days" a whole new meaning. Advertisers, users, and employees each experienced their own levels of anxiety, wonder, sadness, excitement, disgust, and fear about what was likely to happen. As we've seen, all leaders need to grow self-awareness, but once their blind spots are identified, the next job is to get to work on them.

Working with a December 2022 article in *Bloomberg Businessweek* and a *Search Engine Journal* timeline, I pieced together highlights of what took place at Twitter between October 27 and December 2, 2022. In that thirty-seven-day period, Musk closed the deal; reviewed the finances and, finding the company was losing $4 million a day, laid off half the workforce and asked the rest to work "hard-core" twelve-hour shifts; ended Twitter's work-from-anywhere policy; reinstated Donald Trump's account; and shared his vision for "Twitter 2.0." Whew.

What we see in this timeline are three patterns of behaviour. The first is a command-and-control style of leadership, where employees weren't consulted about any of the changes he implemented. I can't help but wonder what critical information Elon might have missed as a result of this approach. How many employees might have stayed had they been made to feel they would have a say in "Twitter 2.0"? For me, the ultimate question is, How much faster and further might Elon have gone if he had been a more integrated relational leader?

The second pattern is reminiscent of what Jeff Martin called "caustic honesty"; not one to candy-coat, Elon's brutal truths left his employees and advertisers reeling. Elon's "Fork in the Road" email (where employees were asked to commit to hard-core work or leave) was a defining moment that changed Twitter's culture and work conditions. Employees were left to make a decision about the kind of place they wanted to work in. Many voted with their feet. Recent Glassdoor ratings give Elon a 12% approval rating as Twitter's CEO.[94]

A third pattern rests in Elon's approach to what's called "innovation as iteration." He is a master at harnessing speed to drive momentum, something all leaders need to pay more attention to. He shared with *Inc.* magazine the three questions that guide his innovation process: "How long will it take you to build? Do you have the right resources? Can you obtain the required raw materials?" If we trace his activities between October 27 and December 2, an equation emerges where "time plus people plus materials equals the ability to innovate."[95]

Elon is an innovator extraordinaire—there's no doubt of that. But here's my question. How many fewer crashes might Tesla have had if he'd listened more? How much more profitable might Twitter be if he collaborated more? Could Twitter have gone from losing $4 million a day to making $4 million a day because he took the time to listen first and then take action? Stay tuned. A helpful way for you to become a more integrated leader is to identify three or four leaders who intrigue you. Put them on your radar screen, and keep following their exploits. Ask yourself, How are they leading? Where are they innovative? When do they run into trouble and why? Keeping up to date with real-world leadership stories is a powerful way to illuminate your own journey.

INCUBATE, LAUNCH, ENTRENCH

The mantra running through this book is that leadership is a way to be, not a thing to do. When we embrace leadership holistically, we not only do good for our company, but we also have the potential to help the world. As a holistic leader, you want to think beyond the workplace. The rise of ESG (environmental, social, and governance) and DEI (diversity, equity, and inclusion) have spurred organizations to redefine leadership and what it means to be profitable and encourage their employees to take on causes that enrich their communities. We see energy companies seeking new ways to harness carbon capture, the automotive industry shifting to electric vehicles, and retailers and sports teams linking up with marginalized populations to build powerful new forms of partnership, sponsorship, and allyship.

A Wharton study on sustainability discovered that it is a misstep for leaders to delegate sustainability to a single unit rather than integrating it throughout the organization.[96] They recommend leaders instead embrace a three-act process, beginning by *incubating* an approach to sustainability. During this stage the organization defines the company's purpose and sets concrete goals. The second act is to *launch* the program to all employees and stakeholders. Finally, leaders *entrench* sustainability practices, seamlessly embedding them in the cultural DNA. We saw an example of this in Unilever's approach to growing their employees' engagement through the development of their purpose story in tandem with efforts to provide a living wage to workers around the world.

When we combine these acts of sustainability with integrative practices, we help construct a better future. But not every act has to be a multimillion-dollar effort. Small acts can have long-lasting effects and can more easily be piloted and then built upon. So don't be intimidated thinking you have to create the next UNICEF. You can do something small but impactful, sponsoring a school breakfast program, helping houseless people in your local community, or supporting a shelter for abused women.

EMBRACE THE INTEGRATOR'S MANTRA: DO WELL BY DOING GOOD

When I interviewed Stephen Letwin, he was the CEO of IAMGOLD, a mining company with locations around the world. He decided to take on this role against the counsel of friends and family. He shared with me: "I wanted to change, I wanted to try something new. I liked the idea of working in Africa and South America. I liked the idea of adding value there. I saw that we could improve the standard of living there and we could build a Canadian company while we did that."

When I asked Stephen about his philosophy of leadership and how it had changed over time, he described his moment of truth:

> I had just landed in Ouagadougou [the capital of Burkina Faso] and was travelling from the airport to the hotel. I saw all of these small campfires along the sides of the road. A lot of young people were around the campfires, and there was one thing I saw that struck me: I saw those phones. I saw light coming from all of these phones. They were like fireflies. It seemed like there were a million cell phones. I thought to myself, "These young people know exactly what's going on. They look at their situation and say, 'Hey, wait a minute. Why am I living in a hut on the side of the road with no bed?'"
>
> And as I looked at that, I thought to myself, "I have to think of my values and my children and grandchildren. Unless we do something, this world is going to get ugly." At the time experts were predicting an increase of two billion more people in the world, and at least half of those will be in Africa in the next thirty years. I asked myself some pretty hard questions: "Where are they going? Where are they getting water? What is the plan for them?"
>
> I can't imagine doing my job without this dimension. I don't think my level of job satisfaction would be anywhere near where it is. And it's very high.

That image of "firefly cell phones" inspired Stephen to create a multimillion-dollar Canadian public-private partnership to improve educational opportunities and provide greater access to job-readiness training for the youth of Burkina Faso. Focused on kids aged thirteen to eighteen, with a strong emphasis on girls, the program provides technical and vocational training and life skills and is expected to double enrolment in secondary education. In recognition of his efforts, Stephen was made an officer of the National Order of Burkina Faso in 2011.

When announced, Stephen's efforts created the largest public-private partnership in Canadian International Development Agency's (CIDA) history. The project was developed in collaboration with local and regional authorities throughout the country. As Stephen describes it, "It was the right thing to do and aligned with our core purpose to enrich the lives of all of our stakeholders."

Stephen's story defines what it means to see possibility and to make a difference. His humility moved him to *incubate* an approach to better understand a complex situation and what he could do to help. We see him *launch* the project by bringing stakeholders together and empowering them to create a program for youth to build a better future. Finally, we see him *entrench* by working with CIDA to pioneer new ways for the company to support young people. He not only helped develop employable skills but also developed an environmental energy program. His story demonstrates that powerful things can happen when commerce and social justice join forces.

Stephen closed our interview by saying, "I will tell you that I'm a better individual, a better leader, after seven years of doing this than I would have been if I had remained in the same job for another seven years. So that risk I took on helped me develop. It changed my life."

PRACTICE BECOMING A SELFLESS LEADER

Here are my seven practices to become a selfless leader:

- **Step 1: Helicopter up.** Ask yourself where you see yourself in ten years. What kind of leadership experiences will you need to get yourself there? Be the architect of your own plan. Don't wait for someone to take charge of your leadership development. Identify people whose skills you admire and link up with them. Invest in your leadership—go to conferences; more importantly, speak at them. There's nothing better to focus the mind than preparing to give a speech on how you got to where you are.

- **Step 2: Remember that leadership is a business issue.** There's no point in working on integrating leadership behaviours if you fail to connect them to your broader objectives. Situate your leadership in your current mission and organizational strategy. Identify the kinds of behaviours required to achieve your strategic goals. Next, identify the hard and soft skills you need to develop. Be honest with yourself: Where are the gaps? Now, get to work closing those gaps methodically and systematically.

- **Step 3: Integrate the seven relational leadership practices.** Identify the two or three areas that you feel you're not using enough. Reflect on moments of truth, and discipline yourself to move from one behaviour to another. An example of this could be "I want to empower others by moving *from* being a lone wolf *to* being a leader who listens more." Enlist a friend or colleague to give you feedback that you can integrate into your new behaviours. As we've seen throughout this book, giving and receiving feedback is fundamental to your growth.

- **Step 4: Model the behaviour.** Now that you've made your assessment of practices you would like to try, share your goals with your team and pledge to get there. Ask them to keep you honest. When you show your team how hard you are working to become more relational, they will do the same. Your story becomes their story. Their story becomes your story.

- **Step 5: Nurture your inherent humility.** Understand where you fit into the ecosystem of your organization: become an astute observer of the world around you; your listening skills need to be as sharp as your observational skills. Use the skills we learned in story making to understand the broader narrative. Cocreate new stories, ones that will be shared, owned, and reshaped to reflect your organization's values.

- **Step 6: Make sustainability a team activity.** Facilitate conversations about ESG and DEI and the kinds of impacts your company could make. Engage in activities across the organization. Break your strategy into short-, medium-, and long-term goals. Stress-test the team's ideas for their potential to have not only an impact on the bottom line but also a positive impact in the community.

- **Step 7: Take action.** Show the way by speaking up. Identify issues that deserve attention. Be prepared with facts and data. Socialize your ideas with key individuals in the organization before you go public. And remember that it's OK to think micro—you don't have to come up with a world-changing innovation, just one small change for good that makes a difference. What mark will you leave?

Evaluate Your Performance

As you contemplate where you would like to leave your mark, respond to these questions:

- How are you developing ways to learn about where you can make a difference?

  _____

  _____

  _____

- What one small change could you make right now to begin leaving your mark?

  _____

  _____

  _____

- Do you have the integrator's number one question—"How can I help?"—always at the top of your mind?

  _____

  _____

  _____

- How do you show up?

- How are you supporting the team to adopt a more relational view?

- How are you ensuring that projects are well resourced?

- How do you intend to invite and engage people of all ages and demographics to join you on the journey? (You can't do it alone!)

- How do you instill and inspire sustainable values, vision, and purpose in your organization's strategy?

  _____

  _____

  _____

- How will you integrate relational practices to ensure you achieve success?

  _____

  _____

  _____

CHAPTER 9

The Compassion Advantage Is Your Competitive Advantage: Begin Your Journey Today

Do you remember me on my knees in the president's office picking up the hundreds of business cards that had fallen to the floor? You might have said to yourself, "Hell, I wouldn't have done that!" Or you might have thought, "You know, she didn't really have a choice; that's just the way it is."

The "business card" story gave me a moment to show you how you can step back and think about your own leadership story from a new perspective. If I were to replay that moment, the human in me would still stoop down to pick up the cards, but the leader in me would now say something like "Hey, can you give me a hand? There's a lot of cards down here!" So simple, right? Keep it light, smile, don't let the moment fester. Throw down a bridge to another human being and look them in the eyes to build a memory together: these are the things relational leadership has taught me. And it's only because I was able to explore them by reigniting my purpose, redefining my values, and developing a new mantra.

We all have a leadership story, a mantra, behaviours that guide how we lead—most of these are unconscious, automatic, and long buried over time. If we don't tend our garden, much like Nelson Mandela did, before we know it, our old stories become weeds choking the plants we've so carefully cultivated over the years.

This is the moment for you to clear out the weeds and establish new growth. This means getting out of your comfort zone, being open to change, and having the courage to look at yourself and others with fresh eyes. We've seen how hard it is to do this—but if we do it right, the rewards are great.

SEE THE LEADER YOU WISH TO BECOME . . . BECOME THAT LEADER

If you and I have done our job well over the past eight chapters, your leadership story has changed. You've changed. And people will notice. As you embrace and deploy these practices, you will recognize change all around you. The drama will begin to die down; team members will become more engaged, loyal, and committed to your shared mission. The team will move faster, make better decisions, and be more productive. Importantly, you will feel less stressed.

But there is one piece of information that I've saved for the end, and it is this: once you sign up to become a relational leader, the journey never ends.

You will need to return again and again to the soul-searching question: "Why did I become a leader in the first place?" These practices should give you the tools to answer that question and remember your purpose.

It takes guts and discipline. Not every innovation will knock it out of the park. There will be moments when you will celebrate failure with your team—but only when it helps promote learning and can lead to new and better things. A disruptive leader doesn't tolerate incompetence. They become relational: when they see teams struggling, they provide people with mentoring, coaching, and the technical skills and risk-taking capabilities to help them flourish. It's their job to help the team get back on their feet after setbacks, to be that guide showing the way.

Relational leaders also need to protect their organizations from one of the most powerful challenges—their past. I work with many organizations that have lived through cost-cutting exercises, restructuring, firings, lawsuits, and critical events. In some cases, these events happened over a decade ago, but they continue to haunt productivity and create a toxic culture. It's up to leadership to break the cycle. By taking the lead to create a new narrative and develop trust, you will inspire people to see a positive future.

As we close out our exploration of relational capabilities, we need to focus on two things that will underpin your success. The first is to embrace these practices to help you see possibility in everything. And with that comes the second: relational leaders are ambassadors of positivity. They can see the light at the end of the longest tunnel, and they know how to wring great learning moments out of even the most abject failure.

BECOME THE COMMUNITY

At a time when many are buckling under the pressure and fatigue of a postpandemic world, we need to stop the complacency that I fear may plague many of us in the coming years. We cannot languish— leaders everywhere need to rethink how they are leading. They need to adopt—and adapt—new practices that address the disruptive times we live in. Leaders who learn to pause, plan, and prepare will be in a much better position to lead stronger, healthier, and more successful teams. As we've seen, the heavy lifting starts with us growing our self-awareness. Smashing the mirror that you may have been long gazing into is the first step to becoming a relational leader. But it's keeping that window open that is work that will never end. As we pick up and model new behaviours along our journey, they show others how to be more open, patient, and compassionate. And with that, we are in a much better position to avoid costly missteps and inspire greater innovation. The coming together of these practices is the heart of the *compassion advantage*. It's what the world is calling for.

KEEP YOUR CUPBOARD FULL

One night I had a very challenging conversation with one of my thesis advisors, Liz Fulop, on the definition of leadership.

You see, I had just read an article that concluded the work of a leader consisted of three things: listening, informal talk, and being cheerful.[97] I couldn't swallow this; there had to be more to it than that. During our Skype meeting that winter night, I said, "Geez, Liz, if that's all there is, the leadership cupboard is pretty bare." Without missing a beat, she countered, saying, "Oh, I think it's pretty full . . ."

Without me knowing it, Liz had just coached me. By each of us sharing our perspective, I was able to pause, check myself, and find new meaning. It was a conversation that "registered." As we grow as leaders, it will be most rewarding to find times like these, when we meet people where they are; you'll know because the conversation clicks, just like ours did. In that tiny moment, Liz had helped me examine my assumptions and rethink almost everything I had thought about leadership. That night a seed was planted that turned into this book.

In that one small moment, I realized that the work is complex but the mission is simple. It is ongoing work; it is challenging work; it engages all our senses and demands the very best of us. But when we do it well, we have the good fortune of feeling fulfilled every day. These are the leaders whose "cupboards are full."

These are relational leaders.

ACKNOWLEDGMENTS

On a snowy Friday night in Toronto in 2009, my husband, Gordon, and I were perched at the bar of our favourite little French restaurant. Through a chance encounter, I became aware of an opportunity to start a PhD at Griffith University in Australia. I was also in the running for a new leadership role. I looked at Gordon and said "Hmm . . . which road to take?" and he said "Why not take both?"

When I think about that night, it was the ultimate moment of truth. My views about what it meant to lead changed dramatically as a result of my walking down both forks in the road. Combined, these experiences allowed me to deeply examine my behaviours and values and pretty well challenged everything I had thought about leadership. I was changed for the better because I had an opportunity to weave the learning with the leading and the leading with the learning. I hope this book has helped you to reflect on your leadership as well as provided you with moments to apply the seven practices to your everyday work experience. But I could have never accomplished any of this without the many people who supported me over the past decade.

The book would never have happened if I hadn't written my PhD thesis first. I'm grateful to Drs. Ngaire Bissett; Liz Fulop, professor emeritus; Sara McGaughey, professor and higher degree research convenor; and Simone Fullagar, associate professor, who encouraged me to go deeper and further in my research than I'd ever thought I could. I so appreciate the work these remarkable women took on as we collaborated between Canadian and Australian time zones, getting to know each other as we practiced the concepts of relational leadership. They taught me to trust the process, and in doing so, we developed a sound trust in each other—a cornerstone of relational leadership.

Once the thesis was completed, I faced the disheartening realization that there was no way it could be turned into a book. It was filled with academic terms that made even my most dedicated fans (my family) fall asleep. Nick Morgan of Public Words encouraged me to interview leaders from all walks of life to bring the research to life, and for that I am grateful.

Although not all thirty-five leaders interviewed appear in the book, their collective insights helped me show you how leadership happens. To those leaders who were kind enough to allow me to publish what were, for some, intense moments of vulnerability, I am deeply indebted: Paul Alofs, Jamie Angell, Diane Brisebois, Ginny Dybenko, Jake Gold, David Goldstein, Kunal Gupta, Wes Hall, Michael Hirsh, Jonathan Kay, Shauna Levy, Jeff Martin, Rob MacIsaac, Alex McLeod, Adria Miller, Marnie Spears, Don Tapscott, Gaëtane Verna, and Wendy Zatylny.

Now that I had real-world experience to demonstrate relational leadership, I was confronted by another painful moment: realizing that the 135,000 words I had written might help cure insomnia but wouldn't be of great help to busy leaders. Luckily my saviour, Christina Henry de Tessan, of Girl Friday Productions, arrived just in time to suggest I work with Emilie Sandoz-Voyer and developmental editors Marni Seneker and Ruthie Ackerman. This dream team was filled with enough tough love to help me put the book on a diet and whip it into shape for the harried, multitasking "just give me the headline" leaders you all are. Paul Barrett created a book design that reflected the relational approach and helped break down the key practice and reflective areas simply and elegantly. Jaye Whitney Debber and Janice Lee performed marvels of editing. Thank you to Sam Michaels, who created the illustrations that provide the visual cues for each of the chapters.

While the professionals' help was brilliant, it was the support of friends that truly made a difference. Thank you to friends Rose and Bill Challenger, Jon Churchill and Cheryl Durand, Ingrid and Barry Norrish, Eleanor and Chris Slawson, Carrie and Lindsay Andrews, Lilo Bulger, Sherry McLaughlin, Chris Bulger, Joan Pajunen, John Torella, Laurie Metrick, Vince Molinaro, Frank Cerisano, Nick Nicolaou, Sue Cockburn, and Kelly McDonald.

The "sanity checks" brought on by my close business colleagues

Heather Phelps, Jayson Phelps, Valerie Phelps, and Heather Angel are much appreciated.

The unconditional love of family proved to be the life raft that brought the book home. Carol and Hank Birch, my parents, read and edited the first full draft of my thesis (all five hundred pages) in the summer of 2014. After Dad passed in 2015, it was Mom who kept urging me to "get the damn book done," and here it is. I only wish she could see it. Cancer snatched that possibility away from us in 2022, but up until the last, Mom was steadfast in her belief that more work was required to help leaders. As I look back, I wonder if it was Mom's early stories about leaders she had worked with—some good, others horrifying—that piqued my interest in leadership to begin with. Thanks also to my brother Glenn—the king of "incoming"—his partner Mia, Vanessa, Colin, and Katelyn. Glenn has said he doesn't read books, prompting the need for an audio version of this book. Thanks, Glenn.

My in-laws, John and Helen Parker, played a vital role in the book's evolution by sharing their own stories of leadership. John, as retired commissioner of the Northwest Territories, continually regaled me with stories of his early pioneering work in seeing through the eyes of others, while Helen, one of the first women ever to sit on the board of one of Canada's national banks, shared her insights on leadership dynamics, power, and privilege.

My son Clayton has had a ringside seat to my leadership and academic journeys. His memories of the never-ending start and stop of early transcription machines, Post-it notes pasted all over the house, and Sunday-night dinners where we talked about the leaders we both admired must have left some impression! He now works with me at our company, helping leaders to be the best they can possibly be. Clayton, you made me the best I could possibly be. Thank you for your support during all those crazy-busy years of work and research.

To my much-loved stepkids, Graeme and Nigel, and their partners, Zena and Karla, and to Victoria and Alyson, a big thanks. They must have thought at times that I'd lost my head as I took over their vacated bedrooms, covering them in mind maps and artifacts to make sense of the research. While Clay was used to it, they endured what must have seemed like endless discussions and ramblings about what I was thinking and what it might mean to the book. Their keen questioning about what the next chapter might look like always gave me pause, allowing me to question and revisit things—perhaps one of the earliest forms of reflexivity I was to experience, but as yet unnamed at that point.

And finally, to Gordon Parker, my dream come true of a husband, who has encouraged me all these years. Little did he know that on that cold winter night he would be getting his own PhD, in patience and resilience! He both encouraged and challenged me to make this book as helpful to leaders as possible. As I mentioned, I'm no artist—but luckily Gordon is. He has been instrumental in the design of this book, humanizing the cover design and the illustration concepts. Through all our time together talking about the book, his support, sense of humour, creativity, and ability to cut to the nub of the most densely complex materials I will likely ever encounter in my life saved me in every way possible.

REFERENCES

1 Ungerleider, Neal. "Does the Internet Dream About Itself? Werner Herzog Wants to Know." *Fast Company*, August 17, 2016. https://www .fastcompany.com/3062829/does-the-internet-dream-about-itself -werner-herzog-wants-to-know.

2 Tapscott, Don. "A New Social Contract for the Digital Economy." Blockchain Research Institute, January 16, 2018. https://www.block chainresearchinstitute.org/project/declaration-of-interdependence/.

3 Bregman, Peter. "How (and Why) to Stop Multitasking." *Harvard Business Review*, July 23, 2014. https://hbr.org/2010/05/how-and-why -to-stop-multitaski.

4 Challenger, Gray & Christmas, Inc. "CEO Turnover Report | Challenger, Gray & Christmas, Inc.," n.d. https://www.challengergray.com/tags /ceo-turnover-report/.

5 Smith, Allen. "Generational Mindsets Affect the Workforce." *SHRM*, September 12, 2021. https://www.shrm.org/resourcesandtools/hr -topics/global-hr/pages/generational-mindsets-affect-workforce.aspx.

6 Goldberg, Emma. "The 37-Year-Olds Are Afraid of the 23-Year-Olds Who Work for Them." *New York Times*, October 28, 2021. https://www .nytimes.com/2021/10/28/business/gen-z-workplace-culture.html.

7 Blackburn, Simon, Jeff Galvin, Laura LaBerge, and Evan Williams. "Strategy for a Digital World | McKinsey." McKinsey Digital, October 8, 2021. https://www.mckinsey.com/capabilities/mckinsey-digital/our -insights/strategy-for-a-digital-world.

8 The Silverado Roundtable. "The Nature of the Post-Pandemic Workplace." n.d. https://planterra.com/wp-content/uploads/2021/01 /Nature-of-the-Post-Pandemic-Workplace-1.pdf.

9   Esimai, Chinwe. "Great Leadership Starts with Self-Awareness." *Forbes*, February 15, 2018. https://www.forbes.com/sites/ellevate/2018/02/15 /self-awareness-being-more-of-what-makes-you-great/#64f73f3640dd.

10   "Women Poised to Effectively Lead in Matrix Work Environments, Hay Group Research Finds." Business Wire, March 27, 2012. https://www .businesswire.com/news/home/20120327005180/en.

11   Carucci, Ron. "Organizations Can't Change If Leaders Can't Change with Them." *Harvard Business Review*, October 24, 2016. https://hbr .org/2016/10/organizations-cant-change-if-leaders-cant-change-with -them.

12   Eurich, Tasha. "What Self-Awareness Really Is (and How to Cultivate It)." *Harvard Business Review*, April 6, 2023. https://hbr.org/2018/01 /what-self-awareness-really-is-and-how-to-cultivate-it.

13   Training Industry, Inc. "The Importance of Self-Awareness in Leadership." *Training Industry*, April 19, 2022. https://trainingindustry.com/articles /leadership/the-importance-of-self-awareness-in-leadership/.

14   Harapyn, Larysa. "Kingsdale Advisors' Wes Hall on Combatting Systemic Racism in Canada." *Financial Post*, June 12, 2020. https:// financialpost.com/news/fp-street/kingsdale-advisors-wes-hall-on -combatting-systemic-racism-in-canada.

15   The Taos Institute. "Ann L. Cunliffe, Ph.D.," February 10, 2023. https:// www.taosinstitute.net/about-us/people/institute-associates/mexico -caribbean-central-south-america/brazil/ann-l-cunliffe.

16   Nelvana Wiki. "Nelvana | Nelvana Wiki | Fandom," n.d. https://nelvana .fandom.com/wiki/Nelvana.

17   Bykunal. "Giving Up Control," February 26, 2023. https://www.bykunal .com/post/control-2.

18   Taylor, Kate, and Chris Hannay. "Power Plant Clashes with Harbourfront Centre, Causing Leadership Vacuum." *Globe and Mail*, September 30, 2022. https://www.theglobeandmail.com/arts/art-and-architecture /article-power-plant-director-harbourfront/.

19   Grant, Adam. "We Should Allow Sad Days, Not Just Sick Days (Transcript)." *Ted.com*, July 27, 2021. Accessed July 21, 2023. https:// www.ted.com/podcasts/worklife/we-should-allow-sad-days-not-just -sick-days-transcript.

20   Reporter, Guardian Staff. "Buccaneers Coach Bruce Arians Fined $50,000 for Slapping Own Player." *Guardian*, January 19, 2022.

https://www.theguardian.com/sport/2022/jan/19/bruce-arians
-slaps-player-andrew-adams-tampa-bay-bucs-nfl.

21 D'Auria, Gemma, Sasha Zolley, and Nicolia Chen Nielsen. "Tuning In,
    Turning Outward: Cultivating Compassionate Leadership in a Crisis,"
    May 1, 2020. https://www.mckinsey.com/business-functions/people
    -and-organizational-performance/our-insights/tuning-in-turning
    -outward-cultivating-compassionate-leadership-in-a-crisis.

22 EY. "EY Study: Workers Feel a Sense of Belonging at Their Workplaces,
    Yet Most Are Uncomfortable Sharing All Aspects of Their Identities,"
    September 12, 2023. https://www.ey.com/en_ro/news/2023/09
    /ey-study-workers-feel-a-sense-of-belonging-at-their-workplaces.

23 Murphy, Kate. "Opinion | Talk Less. Listen More. Here's How." *New York
    Times*, January 9, 2020. https://www.nytimes.com/2020/01/09/opinion
    /listening-tips.html.

24 Chan, Goldie. "5 Reasons Why Compassionate Leadership Is the Key to
    Success." *Forbes*, August 18, 2022. https://www.forbes.com/sites
    /goldiechan/2022/08/18/5-reasons-why-compassionate-leadership-is
    -the-key-to-success/?sh=afd6fcf72ff4.

25 Stratton-Berkessel, R. "The Very First Question—Principle of
    Simultaneity." https://positivitystrategist.org/blog/.

26 Kirby, Jason. "Total Slacker: Remote Work Here to Stay Thanks to a
    Canadian's App. One Potential Spoiler—Microsoft." *Globe and Mail*,
    June 8, 2020. https://www.theglobeandmail.com/business/article-total
    -slack-er-remote-work-here-to-stay-thanks-to-a-canadians-app/.
    Quotation used by permission.

27 McGee, Niall, and Jeffrey Jones. "Inside the Ultrasecretive Exit of CEO
    Mayo Schmidt from Nutrien After Eight Months." *Globe and Mail*,
    March 19, 2022. https://www.theglobeandmail.com/business/article
    -inside-the-ultrasecretive-exit-of-ceo-mayo-schmidt-from-nutrien-after/.

28 McKinsey & Company. "Five Fifty: The Skillful Corporation," January 8,
    2021. https://www.mckinsey.com/capabilities/people-and-organizational
    -performance/our-insights/five-fifty-the-skillful-corporation.

29 Gallup. "State of the American Workplace Report." *Gallup.com*,
    February 19, 2020. https://www.gallup.com/workplace/285818/state
    -american-workplace-report.aspx.

30 Brody, Leonard, KPMG Insights, and KPMG. "The Great Rewrite:
    The Future of Work in an Automated World." *Forbes*, July 19, 2018.

https://www.forbes.com/sites/kpmg/2018/07/19/the-great-rewrite-the
-future-of-work-in-an-automated-world/#4aba8ff01105.

31 Palmer, Kelly. "How to Empower Your Employees to Learn New Technology." *Forbes*, August 8, 2019. https://www.forbes.com/sites /quora/2019/08/08/how-to-empower-your-employees-to-learn-new -technology/?sh=49e931f25f37.

32 "What Is Coaching?" *Performance Consultants*, March 28, 2023. https:// www.performanceconsultants.com/what-is-coaching.

33 International Coaching Federation. "ICF Global Coaching Study," accessed November 13, 2023. https://coachingfederation.org/research /global-coaching-study.

34 Bertolino, Bob. *Effective Counseling and Psychotherapy: An Evidence-Based Approach*. New York: Springer Publishing Company, 2018, 4.

35 Working, Russel. "CEO's Video Series Boosts Morale, Engagement." Ragan Communications, April 10, 2018. https://www.ragan.com /ceos-video-series-boosts-morale-engagement/.

36 SportsRec. "How to Win a Jump Ball in Basketball," October 15, 2019. https://www.sportsrec.com/win-jump-ball-basketball-2331056.html.

37 Maruf, Ramishah. "Better.Com CEO Fires 900 Employees over Zoom." CNN Business, December 6, 2021. https://www.cnn.com/2021/12/05 /business/better-ceo-fires-employees/index.html.

38 Aratani, Lauren. "Better.Com CEO to Take Time Off After Firing Hundreds of Employees over Zoom." *Guardian*, December 12, 2021 https://www.theguardian.com/us-news/2021/dec/10/bettercom-ceo -vishal-garg-time-off-firing-employees-zoom.

39 Barrabi, Thomas. "Better Loses More Execs After CEO Vishal Garg Returns Following Zoom Layoff Meltdown." *New York Post*, February 4, 2022. https://nypost.com/2022/02/04/better-com-loses-more-top -executives-after-ceo-vishal-gargs-zoom-layoff-meltdown/.

40 Unilever. "The Unilever Compass for Sustainable Growth." https://www .unilever.com/files/8f9a3825-2101-411f-9a31-7e6f176393a4/the-unilever -compass.pdf.

41 Unilever. "The Unilever Compass."

42 Eccles, Robert G. "Unilever's Purpose and Sustainability Test of Its Shareholders." *Forbes*, February 10, 2022. https://www.forbes.com /sites/bobeccles/2022/02/10/unilevers-purpose-and-sustainability-test -of-its-shareholders/?sh=128c80093dfb.

43 "Unilever WEF IBC Disclosure Index," accessed July 27, 2023. https://www.unilever.com/files/e7908d4a-8627-47d8-a43a-c4013a435f1c/unilever-wef-ibc-disclosure-index.pdf.

44 Choy, Esther. "Business Storytelling Culture Can Improve Your Organization in 3 Big Ways." *Forbes*, September 19, 2021. https://www.forbes.com/sites/estherchoy/2021/09/19/business-storytelling-culture-can-improve-your-organization-in-3-big-ways/?sh=1edd45744a93.

45 Zak, Paul J. "The Neuroscience of Trust." *Harvard Business Review*, August 31, 2021. https://hbr.org/2017/01/the-neuroscience-of-trust.

46 2023 Edelman Trust Barometer Special Report: The Collapse of the Purchase Funnel." Edelman.com, accessed November 13, 2023. https://www.edelman.com/sites/g/files/aatuss191/files/2023-06/Edelman_BrandTrust_Top10.pdf.

47 Edelman, Richard. "Trust Barometer Special Report: Brand Trust and the Coronavirus Pandemic." Edelman.com, March 30, 2020. https://www.edelman.com/research/covid-19-brand-trust-report.

48 Frei, Frances X., and Anne Morriss. "Begin with Trust." *Harvard Business Review*, May–June 2020. https://hbr.org/2020/05/begin-with-trust#:~:text=In%20our%20experience%2C%20trust%20has,care%20about%20them%20(empathy).

49 Kay, Grace, and Kali Hays. "A Diary of Elon Musk's Totally Chaotic First Week of Owning Twitter." *Business Insider*, November 15, 2022. https://www.businessinsider.com/elon-musk-twitter-takeover-timeline-details-2022-11.

50 "Edelman Trust Barometer 2021," accessed July 27, 2023. https://www.edelman.com/sites/g/files/aatuss191/files/2021-01/2021-edelman-trust-barometer.pdf.

51 "Culture Shift: Changing Beliefs, Behaviors, and Outcomes." Deloitte United States, n.d. https://www2.deloitte.com/us/en/pages/finance/articles/cfo-insights-culture-shift-beliefs-behaviors-outcomes.html.

52 Collinson, David L. "Questions of Distance." *Leadership* 1, no. 2 (June 1, 2005): 235–50. https://doi.org/10.1177/1742715005051873.

53 Jackall, Robert. *Moral Mazes: The World of Corporate Managers*. New York: Oxford University Press, 1988, 56.

54 Juneja, Prachi. "Kurt Lewin's Change Management Model: The Planned Approach to Organizational Change," n.d. https://www.managementstudyguide.com/kurt-lewins-change-management-model.htm.

55 Boris, Vanessa. "What Makes Storytelling So Effective for Learning?"
    Harvard Business Publishing, December 20, 2017. Accessed January 9,
    2023. https://www.harvardbusiness.org/what-makes-storytelling-so
    -effective-for-learning/.

56 Eichenwald, Kurt. "How Microsoft Lost Its Mojo: Steve Ballmer and
    Corporate America's Most Spectacular Decline." *Vanity Fair*, July 24, 2012.
    https://www.vanityfair.com/news/business/2012/08/microsoft-lost
    -mojo-steve-ballmer.

57 "Microsoft CEO Satya Nadella Wants to 'Make Other People Cool,'
    Here's Why." *Financial Express*, February 15, 2019. https://www
    .financialexpress.com/life/technology-microsoft-ceo-satya-nadella
    -wants-to-make-other-people-cool-heres-why-1488007/.

58 Grohl, Dave. "Dave Grohl: The Irreplaceable Thrill of the Rock Show."
    Atlantic, May 11, 2020. Accessed November 22, 2022. https://www
    .theatlantic.com/culture/archive/2020/05/dave-grohl-irreplaceable
    -thrill-rock-show/611113/.

59 "Herbie Hancock Remembers the Time He Played the Wrong Chord
    During a Miles Davis Performance." That Eric Alper, March 18, 2018.
    https://www.thatericalper.com/2018/03/18/herbie-hancock-remembers
    -time-played-wrong-chord-miles-davis-performance/.

60 Kelly, Samantha Murphy. "Former WeWork CEO Adam Neumann Opens
    Up About His Regrets." CNN Business, November 9, 2021. https://www
    .cnn.com/2021/11/09/tech/adam-neumann-wework-regrets.

61 Wingard, Jason. "The WeWork Disaster: Three Signs a Leader's Time Is
    Up." *Forbes*, October 3, 2019. Accessed July 11, 2023. https://www.forbes
    .com/sites/jasonwingard/2019/10/03/the-wework-disaster-three-signs
    -a-leaders-time-is-up/#50d139e75fee.

62 Carroll, Anne M. "Top 10 Main Causes of Project Failure." Project-
    Management.com, October 20, 2022. https://project-management.com
    /top-10-main-causes-of-project-failure/.

63 Kanter, Rosabeth Moss. "Leading Your Team Past the Peak of a Crisis."
    Harvard Business Review, April 30, 2020. https://hbr.org/2020/04/leading
    -your-team-past-the-peak-of-a-crisis.

64 "LISTENING CIRCLE (Approximately 50 Minutes)." Sourcefield, n.d.
    Accessed July 11, 2023. https://sourcefield.network/wp-content/uploads
    /2022/05/Listening-Circle-eng-50min.pdf.

65 Fiske, Susan T., and Patricia W. Linville. "What Does the Schema

Concept Buy Us?" *Personality and Social Psychology Bulletin* 6, no. 4 (December 1980): 543–557. https://doi.org/10.1177/014616728064006.

66 Kaplan, Sarah, and Mary Tripsas. "Thinking About Technology: Applying a Cognitive Lens to Technical Change." BS Technology & Operations Management Unit Research Paper No. 04-039, *SSRN Electronic Journal*, August 23, 2007. https://doi.org/10.2139/ssrn.1008908.

67 Kaplan, "Thinking About Technology."

68 Fredrickson, Barbara L., and Christine Branigan. "Positive Emotions Broaden the Scope of Attention and Thought-Action Repertoires." *Cognition and Emotion* 19, no. 3 (July 19, 2022): 313–332. https://doi .org/10.1080/02699930441000238.

69 Bundrant, Mike. "What Lens Do You Choose?" *Psychology Today*, n.d. Accessed July 11, 2023. https://www.psychologytoday.com/us/blog /your-neurochemical-self/201808/what-lens-do-you-choose.

70 Swartz, Mimi. "How Does Empathy Work? A Writer Explores the Science and Its Applications." *New York Times*, April 24, 2018, sec. Books. https://www.nytimes.com/2018/04/24/books/review/i-feel-you -cris-beam.html.

71 Singh, Harbir, and Scott Belsky. "The Messy Middle: Working Through Your Company's Adolescence." Mack Institute for Innovation Management, October 25, 2018. https://mackinstitute.wharton.upenn .edu/2018/messy-middle-scott-belsky/.

72 Kolata, Gina. "Kati Kariko Helped Shield the World from the Coronavirus." *New York Times*, April 8, 2021, sec. Health. https://www .nytimes.com/2021/04/08/health/coronavirus-mrna-kariko.html.

73 Bar Am, Jordan, Laura Furstenthal, Felicitas Jorge, and Erik Roth. "Innovation in a Crisis: Why It Is More Critical than Ever." McKinsey.com, June 17, 2020. https://www.mckinsey.com/capabilities/strategy-and -corporate-finance/our-insights/innovation-in-a-crisis-why-it-is -more-critical-than-ever.

74 "New Study Reveals Importance of Innovation to Consumers." CustomerThink, July 17, 2015. https://customerthink.com/new-study -reveals-importance-of-innovation-to-consumers/.

75 Christensen, Clayton M., Michael E. Raynor, and Rory McDonald. "What Is Disruptive Innovation?" *Harvard Business Review*, December 2015. https://hbr.org/2015/12/what-is-disruptive-innovation.

76   "Apple Developers Grow App Store Ecosystem Billings and Sales by 24 Percent in 2020." Apple Newsroom (Canada), updated June 2, 2021. Accessed July 11, 2023. https://www.apple.com/ca/newsroom/2021/06/apple-developers-grow-app-store-ecosystem-billings-and-sales-by-24-percent-in-2020/.

77   Keen, Paige. "Paul Alofs." Prezi.com, April 18, 2014. https://prezi.com/8eocjbekqwc0/paul-alofs/.

78   "About." Alexander McLeod, 2023. https://www.alxclub.com/about.

79   "About." Bill O'Connor, n.d. Accessed July 11, 2023. https://www.billoconnor.io/about.

80   Cigelske, Tim. "Thinking like a Kid Is a Superpower." The Creative Journey. Medium, October 21, 2019. https://medium.com/the-creative-journey/thinking-like-a-kid-is-a-superpower-afe1d858545f.

81   Bigman, Dan. "How to See the Future." Corporate Board Member, December 20, 2019. https://boardmember.com/how-to-see-the-future/.

82   Hess, Abigail Johnson. "The Science and Design Behind Apple's Innovation-Obsessed New Workspace." CNBC, September 14, 2017. https://www.cnbc.com/2017/09/13/the-science-and-design-behind-apples-innovation-obsessed-new-workspace.html.

83   Levenston, Michael. "Nelson Mandela- Prisoner, Rooftop Food Gardener." City Farmer News, n.d. Accessed July 11, 2023. https://cityfarmer.info/nelson-mandela-prisoner-rooftop-food-gardener/.

84   Rotberg, Robert. "Opinion: Visionary Leadership in Politics Is All Too Rare." *Globe and Mail*, January 16, 2023. https://www.theglobeandmail.com/opinion/article-visionary-leadership-in-politics-is-all-too-rare/.

85   Braithwaite, Sharon. "Zelensky Refuses US Offer to Evacuate, Saying 'I Need Ammunition, Not a Ride.'" CNN, February 26, 2022. https://www.cnn.com/2022/02/26/europe/ukraine-zelensky-evacuation-intl/index.html.

86   Shuster, Simon. "Inside Zelensky's World." *Time*, April 28, 2022. https://time.com/6171277/volodymyr-zelensky-interview-ukraine-war/.

87   Shuster. "Inside Zelensky's World."

88   Shuster. "Inside Zelensky's World."

89   Hernandez, Morela, Jasmien Khattab, and Charlotte Hoopes. "Why Good Leaders Fail." *MIT Sloan Management Review*, April 12, 2021. https://sloanreview.mit.edu/article/why-good-leaders-fail/.

90   Cox, Christopher. "Elon Musk's Appetite for Destruction." *New York*

Times, January 17, 2023. Accessed July 21, 2023. https://www.nytimes
.com/2023/01/17/magazine/tesla-autopilot-self-driving-elon-musk.html.

91   "How Elon Musk's Satellites Have Saved Ukraine and Changed Warfare."
Economist, January 5, 2023. https://www.economist.com/briefing/2023
/01/05/how-elon-musks-satellites-have-saved-ukraine-and-changed
-warfare.

92   Metz, Cade. "Elon Musk Backtracks, Saying His Company Will Continue
to Fund Internet Service in Ukraine." *New York Times*, October 15, 2022.
https://www.nytimes.com/2022/10/15/world/europe/musk-ukraine
-internet-starlink.html.

93   Cox. "Elon Musk's Appetite for Destruction."

94   Manager, Former Employee. "What Is Twitter? Company Culture, Mission,
Values." Glassdoor, accessed July 27, 2023. https://www.glassdoor.ca
/Overview/Working-at-Twitter-EI_IE100569.11,18.htm.

95   Main, Kelly. "Elon Musk Reveals His Innovation Equation. It's an Easy
Way to Gauge If a Business Idea Is Viable." *Inc.*, March 29, 2022. https://
www.inc.com/kelly-main/elon-musk-reveals-his-innovation-equation-its
-an-easy-way-to-gauge-if-a-business-idea-is-viable.html.

96   "Sustaining Sustainability: How Small Actions Make a Big Difference."
Knowledge at Wharton, December 13, 2019. https://knowledge.wharton
.upenn.edu/article/small-actions-big-difference/.

97   Alvesson, Mats, and Stefan Sveningsson. "Managers Doing Leadership:
The Extra-Ordinarization of the Mundane." *Human Relations* 56, no. 12
(December 2003): 1435–1459. https://doi.org/10.1177
/00187267035612001.

ABOUT THE AUTHOR

© Matthew Plexman, Plexman Studio

Dr. Jill Birch has devoted her life to helping leaders and teams realize their vision and achieve strategic goals by developing exceptional leadership. Through the development of the relational leadership framework, as well as other programs and keynotes, she is a collaborator and thinking partner supporting clients to identify and then act on the kinds of leadership required to fulfill their mission and strategy.

As a leader, Birch has been a CEO and member of several C-suites; as a consultant, she helps other leaders become more confident, caring, and future facing. As an academic, she has done ten years of pioneering research in relational leadership, ensuring that leaders receive the benefit of working with an expert who is constantly learning. She is the founder and CEO of DrJillBirch.com, where she helps for-profit and not-for-profit organizations across many sectors. With an MA from the University of Toronto and a PhD from Griffith University in Australia, Birch has spoken to thousands of leaders around the world about fostering teamwork, building engagement, and creating the right metrics to measure success. Learn more at DrJillBirch.com

Printed in the USA
CPSIA information can be obtained
at www.ICGtesting.com
LVHW091244250624
783958LV00012B/39/J

9 781738 102938